Rise!

Creating Unlimited Happiness
and Success
by Overcoming Our Barriers

By Tim Schneider

Dedicated to all the people, who like me, know they have some work to do on themselves, and are willing to embrace that process, and to all the people who want more in life, more happiness, and maybe more success.

Also dedicated to my long-time companion, Sydney the Corgi. I know you will have a ball in your mouth when I see you again and thank you for all of your loyalty, laughs, and love. Frap on my girl.

Printed in the United States of America
First Printing, 2024
Second Edition, N/A

ISBN: 978-0-9982198-0-6
Library of Congress Control Number: 2024920321
Aegis Learning LLC, Publisher
www.discoveraegis.com
info@discoveraegis.com

Ordering Information:
Quantity sales. Special discounts are available on quantity purchases by wholesalers, corporations, associations, and others. For details, contact the publisher at the address above.

Disclaimer:

This book is presented solely for educational and personal development purposes. The author and publisher are not offering it as legal, accounting, or other professional services advice. While best efforts have been used in preparing this book, the author and publisher make no representations or warranties of any kind and assume no liabilities of any kind with respect to the accuracy or completeness of the contents and specifically disclaim any implied warranties of merchantability or fitness of use for a particular purpose. Neither the author nor the publisher shall be held liable or responsible to any person or entity with respect to any loss or incidental or consequential damages caused, or alleged to have been caused, directly or indirectly, by the information or programs contained herein. No warranty may be created or extended by sales representatives or written sales materials. Every person and organization are different, and the advice and strategies contained herein may not be suitable for your situation. You should seek the services of a competent professional before beginning any improvement program. The story and its characters and entities are fictional. Any likeness to actual persons, either living or dead, is strictly coincidental. No artificial intelligence (AI) was used to produce any portion of this book.

"Rise! Creating Unlimited Happiness and Success by Overcoming Our Barriers" by Tim Schneider is a powerful guide for anyone seeking personal growth and success. Tim's ability to break down complex self-limiting behaviors and offer actionable insights makes this book both inspiring and practical. His conversational tone and engaging storytelling draw readers in, making the journey of self-improvement feel approachable and achievable. Whether you're looking to unlock more happiness or overcome obstacles that hold you back, *Rise!* provides the tools and encouragement to take that next step. A must-read for anyone committed to becoming their best self.

Rod Streets, Chief Financial Officer

Tim Schneider has done it again. Using his unique, conversational writing style and deep insight into human behavior, RISE! is another must read from Tim's pen that will serve as a remarkable tool to move all readers from good to great. Understanding the barriers to success and happiness and how to overcome them provides the perfect impetus to do something about them and overcome them.

Steve Buuck, Ph.D., CEO, Faith Lutheran Middle School & High School

Tim's no-nonsense approach to personal growth is refreshing. He uses practical examples to demonstrate the concepts, which makes his advice easy to digest and implement right away. Rise is a must-read for anyone looking to invest in their personal growth. It's packed with practical examples that teach you how to not only better yourself, but be a more impactful, successful leader. Rise is packed with useful nuggets of information that can quickly transform your personal growth journey and take your leadership skills to the next level.

Lisa Kalkes, Chief Marketing Officer

Tim has done it again! Rise hits to the core, tells it like it is, and provides practical advice, strategies, and approaches that any executive can implement immediately and get results. What always impresses me about Schneider is how he takes his vast, practical experience from his hands-on work with thousands of executives and synthesizes it into easy-to-understand, accessible lessons. Tim's wisdom is among the best that I've seen from my experience spanning Harvard Business School, years at McKinsey & Company, and as a Fortune 500 executive at Goodyear, PepsiCo, and NCR.

Eric Berg, CEO & Founder,
AspenView Technology Partners, Inc.

I have had the opportunity to sit in a room full of leaders-in-training while Tim wittingly unlocked insights into life, business, as well as myself. He has an engaging training style in which there is a clear sense of purpose and care. He knows his audience. You may think that you're a great leader already, but don't be fooled; he can see right through you. There is always more to learn, and Tim's goal is to make you the best leader you can be. He knows when you've "got it", but more importantly, he knows that you can "got it" more and he will make sure to take you on the road of learning to get you there. Rise! takes you on that path. Tim's way of conveying the message in this book is fun. At the same time his sage words will hit you over the head. Again, there is always more to learn. You can always be a better person and a better leader.

Karina Tarnowska, Airport Executive

The notions of being a leader and the ability to be an effective leader are different, and Tim's unique training approach to the latter drives home the importance of having the right attitude and not allowing self-limiting behaviors to determine your value and abilities. I learned so much through Tim's various trainings about the importance of being consistent, bringing you're A game every day (if you don't have it in you a particular day, may be a good day to work remote), and using a positive energy to set the tone and guide the ship. I have applied his teachings to greatly enhance my ability to understand and relate to friends, family, and colleagues, and his lessons are now a core part of my leadership style.
Andrea Davis, CEO Viticus Group

Tim is an excellent no nonsense leadership coach who ensures that you hear what you need to hear. In Rise! Tim concisely shares his unique no nonsense guidance via extremely practical suggestions for how to overcome our most dangerous self-defeating behaviors and attitudes. While none of these simple lists may seem terribly complicated, these practical reminders are exactly the sort of nudges that I regularly need to maintain my own quest toward the best version of myself.
Geoffrey Boyce, CEO and Board Member

Contents

Acknowledgements

I am a true believer that people come into our lives and connect with us at exactly the perfect time. No one's appearance was more important to me, and immediately became more valuable than Kristel. Your contributions to this work are immeasurable through the brainstorming, idea vetting, and long conversations. Thank you for making this an amazing year. I love you.

My boys are awesome. Not perfect, just awesome. Thank you, Chris and Matt, for your continued support, cheerleading, and encouragement. You two are the best.

Kelley did an awesome job on the forward for this book, and I am very appreciative of that and all her contributions to Aegis Learning.

Danielle was terrific as an editor and proofreader for RISE! In the later stages of the creation, she became a valued partner, and her margin comments were priceless. Thank you, Danielle.

A big thank you to Rod, Steve, Karina, Eric, Lisa, Geoffrey and Andrea for previewing the book and the very kind comments.

The customers of Aegis Learning are an amazing group of people. People that appreciate growth, challenge, and learning. People that are interested in relationships and not just transactions. People who trust us with their most valuable resource, their people. Thank you is not nearly enough.

Deep appreciation and respect for Dr. Marshall Goldsmith for pioneering the work in self-defeating behaviors. More about his contributions just a bit later.

And final and lasting appreciation for:

Kelley Reynolds	Forward
Danielle Weibel	Editing and Proofreading
Arishah	Cover and Back Design

To my valued readers:

First and foremost, thank you for buying and reading this work. It truly has been a passionate pursuit to put this together and hopefully, make it useful. As always, I appreciate your feedback and welcome any comments you may have.

I am optimistic that this book will find its audience. It is my sincere wish that it will help people; help you. I wanted to gather the information necessary to help people overcome their obstacles and self-sabotage. I want you to be the best you that you can be. I want you to be the happiest you can be. I want you to be the most successful you can be. I want you to have the best relationships and be a magnet for other awesome people. I truly do. It is my hope and my prayer for you. It is my genuine wish that it helps you and many other people. Selfishly, I also want this to be a work in which the people in my life can be proud and say "hey, I know that guy."

For the past 30-plus years, I have had, and continue to have, the best job in the world. I have the distinct privilege of working with thousands of people in all stages of their career and in all industries. I have worked extensively with leadership and executive coaching and that has provided me with insight into behaviors that are self-defeating as well and why those people struggle to change them. This work and the dutiful notes taken during these coaching interactions have provided me, and therefore you, with a great list of self-sabotaging behaviors and stunting beliefs. Their work and struggles have now become your guide.

Like all meaningful work, this was not done alone or in a vacuum. I must acknowledge the work of Dr. Marshall Goldsmith that introduced the world to self-defeating behaviors. I strive to not add to his work but to compliment it in some way.

Danielle Weibel made substantial contributions during the editing phase of this book. She quickly became a valuable partner in the production of this work and her encouragement was very much appreciated.

The other significant contributor to this work is Kristel Vesch. Throughout the construction of this book, she has been an invaluable source of idea vetting and inspiration. Those conversations were rich, challenging, and sometimes difficult, but always valuable to the formation of this work.

You will note that I am not a writer by trade. My tendency is to write as I speak. What you miss in writing spit-and-polish, I hope you glean in substance and usefulness.

Again, thank you for reading and I look forward to hearing about your successes.

Tim

Forward – By Kelley Reynolds

Note: Kelley Reynolds is a gifted and talented facilitator and a member of the Aegis Learning team for the past six years.

I met Tim in a setting similar to many of his students, a conference room filled with the eager or the recalcitrant; those excited to learn something new and those who were voluntold to attend. My then leader hired Tim as part of a succession plan for our department; with the intent to develop relationships and trust among a newly formed team. As the weeks went on, instead of thinking about all the items on my to-do list I should be completing, I would anticipate the class meetings, excited about what were we going to learn this week. During the sessions there would be the pain of realization, but it would soon give way to the excitement of growth and confidence of learning strategies to become a better leader.

Tim is not for the faint of heart. Tim will engage you. His style is distinctive. There is no hiding in a make-believe foxhole from Tim's dry wit and quips.

Tim's unique storytelling style comes to life through the pages. He is driven by a strong desire to help turn managers into leaders; to make work a happier place. He strives to help people become better versions of themselves and in the process to make organizations more desirable places to work. Most importantly, his process provides you with tools to strengthen all of your relationships: at work, at home and in the mirror. As you read this book, Tim will inspire you to improve, to take an honest look at yourself, to be brave enough to see yourself as others do and not simply through the narrative you have created for yourself.

Prior to the COVID pandemic, Tim's classes and coaching were conducted almost entirely in-person. NO POWERPOINT. Just Tim and a room full of people. Driven by Tim's desire to be of service when people needed him most, within two weeks of the shutdown, Tim completely pivoted. He mastered on-line learning platforms, translated the program to PowerPoint and offered help and hope during those uncertain times. He offered this series of seminars free of charge showing me his mastery of leadership skills.

I was deeply honored to stand beside Tim as he navigated some challenges and watch his grace and humility as he looked inward instead of out; calling upon his own strength, searching for answers which created opportunities for growth instead of seeking hollow comfort in blame and denial. Tim, ever the consummate leader, exemplified the best leadership qualities in difficult times. Tim's personal growth through his challenges reveal his character and his propensity to practice what he preaches. He displays a readiness to grow and adapt when the environment changes, to boldly face the new reality and embrace rather than squander opportunities brought about by rapid change.

There is something in this book for everyone. Whether you are embarking on your leadership journey, have a desire to improve your game, are considering at the next wrung or seeking more satisfying relationships, this book is for you. The contents of this book will not simply share with you the "what," Tim also provides you with the "how."

As you read this book, you may experience some cringeworthy moments when you realize: "I did that?" Instead, you and thousands of past readers and attendees are empowered to say to yourself: "I can do this!" Know that you are encouraged and supported to do both. Take the lessons in leadership learned here and pay it forward to the next generation of team members and leaders in your organization, friends and family.

Kelley Reynolds

Section I – Here We Are

Preface

So here we are.

Not sure where here is and it is different for all of you. Here is just the reference to the current point in time and your current condition.

The purpose of this book is to truly unlock the potential that you possess. If you can imagine it, dream it, you can make it happen.

We have limitless ability within us but rarely even scratch the surface of those talents, skills, and aptitudes. Every successful person has confronted limiting beliefs and behaviors at one point, and some do this consistently.

But..................you're happy, healthy, and have everything you want. What could you possibly need to unblock?

Much more on that later but I will pose a few questions for you to ponder:

> 1. Would you value greater happiness or more consistent happiness in your life?

2. Would you appreciate the ability to continue to achieve your success more easily, with less grinding?

3. Would you like to obtain your dream job or perhaps work for yourself?

4. Would you like to be a better role model for others?

5. Would you like to make the lives of those that work for you more satisfying and enjoyable?

6. Would you like higher quality and more meaningful relationships with others?

7. Would you like to explore your unlocked potential?

If there was a yes to any of those, and more likely a few of them, please keep reading.

The other and more subtle purpose of this book is to cause some pause and reflection.

Like many of you, I saw the movie The Sixth Sense a couple of times and then berated myself for not seeing the signs that the Bruce Willis character was already dead. I did the same thing with oranges in The Godfather. Really disappointed with myself that I didn't see the obvious signs and clues. Hopefully, I didn't ruin any movie plots for you.

That type of pause and reflection can be healthy and needed for us. It allows us to look back just a bit and say, "why didn't I?" This should not be a point that you stay fixated upon, but it should be a great and powerful reminder of the impact of limiting and defeating behaviors and attitudes. We can't stay in this spot of "what if" but it does remind us of the prices paid for the things that hold us back.

And finally, an additional purpose of this writing is to provide you with a tool for self-coaching and self-improvement. Not that sitting with me in your office twice a month, or weekly via a virtual meeting isn't appealing, but this can help you in the absence of some professional guidance.

To borrow Jim Collins' phrase for a moment; this is about moving from good to great. From satisfied to truly happy. From working to achieving. From grinding out a living to succeeding.

Credit Where Credit is Due

Dr. Marshall Goldsmith is a legend. An icon. The coaches' coach.

Goldsmith pioneered the work on self-defeating and limiting behaviors with his wildly successful book "What Got You Here Will Not Get You There". This best seller, which was originally published in 2007, is a foundational work that lays out the case to challenge our self-defeating behaviors and confront our ability to change. We have used his work for decades in coaching and training with our customers.

This book does not pretend to expand on Dr. Goldsmith's work or to add anything to his book. There will be some commonality with some of the behaviors and even some strategy elements.

I will always recommend that you read "What Got You Here Will Not Get You There".

Backstory

I have been truly blessed during my last 30-plus years of work. I have had and continue to have the best seat in the house to observe human behavior, learning, growth, and limiting actions. Add to that experience, thousands of hours of research related to behavior, skill building, and associated neuroscience.

My work has allowed me to interact individually with thousands of people, mostly in a leadership role, and tens of thousands more in group sessions. This perspective has granted me the ability to identify, analyze, document, and work through a broad spectrum of self-defeating and self-limiting behaviors and those beliefs and attitudes that hold people back from what they could truly become.

The people that we have interacted with and worked with come from every demographic imaginable. They are c-suite leaders, line-level blue-collar employees, emerging leaders, experienced managers, administrative professionals, doctors, and lawyers. Every industry has been touched on including hospitality, medical, manufacturing, construction, consumer services, and government. The most interesting categorization however is the degrees of traditionally measured success in which we are proud to call our customers. We have worked with name brand companies, billionaires, millionaires, founders, investors, and those who are successful by any measure.

One common thread that all our participants have in common is that they all have at least one, and more likely several, limiting behaviors or beliefs. That's right, even billionaires have some defeating and limited behaviors. Even the always-happy yoga instructor has a few. The perfect couple has some. And when people can identify and overcome them, they achieve levels of success and happiness they didn't realize was possible.

Categorizing people is never fair or accurate, but my experience has also allowed me to identify some populations and group their collective defeating beliefs and behaviors. There are even categories for those that seek coaching and self-improvement and those who don't.

There are those people that believe that training and coaching is for the broken and rolled out only when issues exist and there should be a fix applied. Although there are some benefits to this, the global or organizational gains are nominal. Often in these types of environments, the leaders prescribe training for everyone else but not themselves.

Then there are those who seek learning and growth when things are going well, and they are either at an upswing in their career and life or sitting at a pinnacle point and want to see if there is more. These are the people and, ultimately, the places that they work, that are truly successful in the long term. They are also the people that find great joy and happiness in the continual challenge of growth.

Introduction

Limiting behaviors and beliefs are those things that hold us back from being everything that we want to be. They are the obstacles to our true potential and stunt our growth, success, and many times, our happiness.

We all have them. Rich, poor, old, young, end of career, beginning of a career, leader, team member, it doesn't matter. We all have some of them or many of them. Some are known to us and others are blind spots (known by others but not by ourselves) in our behavior or personality.

When we begin the process of identifying them, gauging, and measuring the impact, and then applying curative actions, we immediately see changes that we desire. As this sounds simple and quick, it is neither. It is easy to understand but much more difficult to fix.

The Enemy Resides on Top of Our Shoulders

The enemy to achieving what we truly want and ultimately, our happiness, rests squarely on the top of our shoulders and at the end of our neck. It will be challenging to combat an enemy that has an outpost between our ears.

Our limitations are self-imposed. Yes, we made them up. Sometimes, they can be evidence based, but most likely, they are the result of our own thoughts that converted to actions and those actions that became habits.

The first challenge will be to identify which of our habits, behaviors and thought patterns serve us well, and we want to keep, then to actively and intentionally dispose of those that are limiting or destructive. This doesn't sound particularly daunting but many limiting behaviors and beliefs masquerade as being useful. Some have been useful either at a point in time or situationally, however the utility of them has long since passed. Even the current successful habits and behaviors can stunt our ability for further and greater growth.

Another challenge for us will be to confront our unwillingness to change. Not everyone is highly change resistant, but all of us have some resistance to the new and different. That lack of motivation to change is explained and detailed further in the next section.

The Two by Four, Elephant in the Room and 800 Pound Gorilla

Success is a powerful intoxicant. Comfort is even more addictive and stupefying. Complacency is a coma.

When we begin experiencing success, especially in the workplace, we start losing our desire to grow and change. Consider this example:

> After 90 days of employment, Emily receives a glowing review for her work. After a full year, she receives another review with near-perfect scores and great comments about her ability to perform the core functions of her job. This cycle repeats for three years and after that, she is offered a supervisory position because of her great work.
>
> And again, after another couple of years, Emily is offered a management position after receiving great reviews and even bonuses.
>
> Now, at her five-year anniversary, after experiencing unbridled success and being praised for all her work, what is her motivation to challenge herself and grow her skills?

In the above example you can certainly give Emily the benefit of the doubt and believe that she has been consistently growing herself and her skills during this process. You can also, and almost equally assume that there has been little or no motivation to push herself through change because everything is going well. In both cases you can be right.

Let's look at Emily Part 2:

> Again, Emily is performing admirably and receiving praise and great reviews for her work. Her company has offered her a promotion, largely based on her longevity and technical skills but not on her ability to lead other people.
>
> Instead of challenging herself to grow and change her skillset to meet the new demand of being a supervisor, Emily continues to do what she has always done. Afterall, it was her prior performance that got her the job, and everyone loved that.

And another example:

> Susan and Ed have been married for ten years and have two beautiful children. They live in a home that by their parents' standards would be a mansion. They possess all the creature comforts that any family would ever need. They have savings, retirement money and can travel when and where they choose.
>
> Motivation to change anything? Any desire to do things differently?

In both examples, the drive and desire to change and grow is greatly diminished by the current level of success.

Now consider this:

Todd is struggling at work. He doesn't think his boss likes him and his last several performance reviews have not been good. A person in human resources openly smirked when he asked about growth and promotional opportunities. He has heard that there may be layoffs and that he may be targeted in that move.

Do you think Todd would be willing to challenge how is has been doing things? Do you think Todd would be open to a change that may facilitate some positive outcomes?

And an example from family life:

Macy and Chris are struggling. Every interaction is tense and there is a heaviness in the home that is easily felt and sensed. The finances of the family are not horrible but certainly could be better. The kids, and even the dogs, know that something is not right. Stupid little things become arguments, there is limited and fragmented communication.

If there were a couple of things that this couple could change, do you think they would jump at the opportunity?

My dad had a favorite anecdote when describing someone who was stubborn or maybe not getting the messages received. He said it was like needing to use a two by four (wood beam) to get the attention of a mule. Now before you write letters to PETA about my long-gone father, consider the visual of someone so stubborn and intrenched in their behaviors that they won't consider changing unless a highly traumatic event thumps them square across the head. Sadly, it's often only when this occurs that some people choose to look inwardly and make the needed changes in their behavior. Challenges and failure make us pliable and eager to learn new ways and lose old habits that created this path. Conversely, success often blinds us to some behaviors and attitudes that hold us back and prevent additional success and greater happiness.

That is not to say that you should avoid comfort and not celebrate when you are comfortable or successful, but that should never be the stopping point. Temporary comfort should yield quickly to ongoing growth and challenge.

The cycle should look like:

Growth
Success
Comfort and Celebration
Growth
Success
Comfort and Celebration
(continues)

And not look like:

Growth
Success
Comfort and Celebration
Continuation of Comfort
Complacency

Blame, Excuses, and Justifications

To get the most from the guidance in this book, and others like it, we must own our behaviors, attitudes, and beliefs. What will not work is blaming, excuse making, denials, or justifications. You will never conquer your self-limiting or self-defeating behaviors if you cannot first acknowledge that they are yours and you created them. Blame is an especially dangerous roll of the roulette wheel.

I am fortunate to have several friends and people close to me that are exceptional at owning their own behavior, their part in struggles, and even their part of disagreements and arguments. Some of them have gone through a lot of things which would have buckled lesser people. But the separation piece with these people is that they own each situation and tackle it as it comes. No blaming of others, although some of that would certainly be justifiable, no excuse making, no denying their ownership of the issues, even if it's minor. They own their part and are open about it. They are a model of the ability to grow and overcome because they first chose to own the behaviors, attitudes, and beliefs. They thoughtfully and intentionally analyze their own behavior and approach.

Conversely, I have had the displeasure of knowing people who have not as much as stepped on a sidewalk crack. All their issues, and there are quite a few, are the fault of ex-spouses, bosses, parents, children, the economy, a sitting president, society, ad nauseam. The reason they remain stuck and unable to move forward is primarily due to the lack of ownership of any of her behaviors that created or contributed to their issues. To them, each person and relationship is disposable upon the first opportunity to blame. Do you remember the circa 2000 song from Shaggy, "It Wasn't Me"?

Excuses and justifications have the same impact as blame. When we create an excuse for why we have a particular behavior, we fail to take ownership in that behavior. When we credit one of our attitudes or beliefs to our environment, we are failing to own it. And as a small side note, a justification, no matter how valid in your mind, sounds like an excuse to even the most empathetic listener. So, your behavior is not because of where you work, where you were born, or any societal customs. Your attitudes are not a creation of work volume, stress at home, or your choice of religious affiliation.

One piece of powerful self-awareness is to examine what part you played in any outcome. View your role. Did you help or hurt the situation? Did your actions make things better or worse? At a minimum, did you facilitate the continuation of a problem?

In practicum this means that your behavior is not because you were in law enforcement for 20 years. Your attitude is not because you were raised by Depression Era parents. Your beliefs are not because you were a lifelong banker. You chose them and, in some cases, chose to perpetuate them long after their shelf life.

Before you go much farther, take a few moments to reflect on your ownership of behaviors, attitudes, and beliefs and subordinate the desire to blame, justify or make excuses.

Self-Honesty and Awareness

Another hint for getting the value from this book is about self-honesty and a true awareness of who you are. This sounds simple enough, but it is much harder than it seems.

We humans are judgmental creatures. We can see, register, and note things that are different, and in our view wrong, with other people in a snap. We do this thousands of times a day. Some of it is based on how someone looks, some of it is how they communicate or talk, some of it is based on their behaviors, but it is all done automatically and quickly. Withholding judgement of others is a discipline that not many people have mastered.

When it comes to seeing our own challenges, limiting behaviors, and defeating beliefs we suddenly go blind. Consider a biblical reference from Matthew, chapter 7, verse 3:

> "Why do you look at the speck of sawdust in your brother's eye and pay no attention to the plank in your own eye? How can you say to your brother, 'Let me take the speck out of your eye,' when all the time there is a plank in your own eye? You hypocrite, first take the plank out of your own eye, and then you will see clearly to remove the speck from your brother's eye."

The admonition in this parable is clear. We clearly see the flaws in others yet do not see them in ourselves.

We all craft a mental narrative of who we believe we are. This is based partially on historical information, some feedback from others (that tends to be the positive versions only), and largely based on who we would like to be or how we would like to be seen. The connection to the truth and this narrative is small with most people, and non-existent with some.

The bottom line is that we don't know ourselves nearly as well as we could or should and this leads to a challenge to become self-honest. Self-honesty requires the admission that you are not what you believe that you are and there are both very good characteristics of you and challenging ones as well. It requires we must look in the mirror and acknowledge the balanced scorecard that comprises our behavior. We are not as good as we think and not nearly as bad as we think sometimes either. We are humans with great value and some limits and defeating elements that can be addressed.

For me, that means I am not nearly as funny as I think I am.

To be open to self-honesty will allow you to see the possibilities of limiting and defeating behaviors and attitudes that come just a bit later.

You Are Not Stuck

A lot of people comment that they are stuck in a certain set of behaviors, beliefs, or habits.

My answer is as simple as I am.

You are not stuck. No one is. Stuck implies the inability to move or change your position. You absolutely have the ability to change and move but sometimes you will need a little help.

If, like me, you grew up in a four-season climate geography, you probably spent some time in a snow drift or mud, and unable to move your vehicle. You were stuck. But along came a tow truck or a group of friends with shovels, and Shazam! you were back moving again.

Our personal and professional growth can often take that same trajectory. Moving along nicely and suddenly we find ourselves sideways in a snowbank. It sure looks like you're stuck but it is only a temporary obstacle if you utilize the help available.

This book is your tow truck.

The Target

From surviving to thriving. From complacent to engaged and energized. From satisfied to happy. From happy to happier than you have ever been. From being good to being great. From an unknown legacy to one that is guaranteed to be memorable.

Ultimately, what we are targeting and shooting for is for you to be happy. And perhaps happier than you have ever been.

What drives individual happiness is, well, very individual. Some will look for more money. Others will look for promotions or a particular job title. And still others will look towards things like location, jumping into entrepreneurialism, better relationships with others, or being a more admired leader. Maybe a winery in Napa is your thing. Perhaps your dreams center around travel.

The exact target doesn't matter but what is important is to achieve an improved state or condition. To be better tomorrow than you were today. To have more happiness moving forward without the stress you are currently feeling.

If you were hoping for a formula to create a million dollars in the next 90 days, I'm sorry. It's not here. Can you create and execute that formula after removing your obstacles and limitations? Absolutely you can.

Behaviors

Our definition of behavior differs slightly from the classical definition. Typically, behavior is defined as how someone acts, especially towards others.

For the context here, a behavior is an outwardly observable action. Something that can be seen or sensed by others.

Some easy examples of behavior include your body language and facial expressions, tone of your voice, fidgeting with your hands, praising others, friendliness, assertiveness, listening abilities, and walking pace. All observable and all actions.

Many of our behaviors are quite useful for us and some can become limiting or defeating. A few behaviors appear to be valuable but are masking a limiting or defeating behavior.

In the short term, behaviors can be very easy to change. If I ask you to smile, you will and probably will for the duration of our interaction. If you learn to be more thankful and practice gratitude, your behaviors and mindset will shift, for a while at least. Long term behavioral change will require more work and examination of deeper elements of why the behavior exists.

Habits

Behaviors that are done repetitively often become habits. Neuroscientists have described a three-part habit loop that includes a cue or trigger, the routine of repeating a behavior, and then a reward, usually intrinsic, that supports the use of the habit.

We all understand habits related to smoking or drug use, but we rarely associate common verbal responses, for example when we look at email, what applications we use on our phones, or other work routines as habits. Again, there are some great habits and some that can be quite limiting. Behaviors or actions typically take 18 to 21 repetitions to become a habit. Likewise, it will take that many repetitions to establish new and more useful habits.

One of our challenges will be to unlearn the automatic responses of habits. Learning the new is relatively easy. Unlearning old habits, especially if they have served you well previously, can be daunting. Not impossible, just a challenge. All of this will start with one habit changed at a time. One step by one step. Much more on that later.

Attitudes and Beliefs

Attitudes and beliefs are complex sets of thoughts that drive our behaviors.

Our attitudes and beliefs drive our behaviors.

Have you ever received a compliment about your "good attitude" about something? It is very likely you have. Did that person have a deeply mystical connection into your soul to see your attitude or were they evaluating your behaviors at that moment? Conversely, have you ever had someone inquiry to see if you were in a "bad mood" or had a "bad attitude" about something? Again, there is a high likelihood that you have. Were they able to see your attitude aura or were they measuring and assessing your behaviors projected by that attitude? Even an inquiry into if we are feeling okay can give insight into the power that attitudes have on our behavior.

Consider these two examples:

> Juan is dreading a meeting. Historically it has been a waste of time and nothing but updates from other departments and lots of longwinded presentations that don't interest him. He has created an attitude of negative expectation. This attitude affects his body language, tone, and overall engagement during the meeting. He is sitting with a scowl on his face, arms

crossed and does not offer any input or appreciation for the updates. And everyone in the room sees it. His attitude has driven these behaviors.

Sonya is looking forward to the same meeting and the opportunity to hear from her peers. She has always enjoyed knowing more about other areas of the company and how they contribute to her success and the overall success of the company. She has created an attitude of positive expectation, and it shows. Her body language is open, she smiles frequently, interjects, and praises the updates. And everyone sees it.

I know this is too simple, be Sonya, not Juan.

Consider a personal example of the relationship between attitude and behavior:

You and your husband are hosting a dinner party, and he has invited a friend of his that you just do not like. You have been thinking about it all day and created an attitude of expectation of a negative outcome. During the gathering, you are sullen, non-communicative, and look like you would rather be anywhere else. Rather than focusing on enjoying the party, the focus was on a particular person. This poorly placed focus caused a negative attitude and experience.

An attitude is a set, or settled, way of thinking about a person, thing, or situation. It is a set of thoughts chained together to create judgement about someone or something. Often these are rooted in some past experiences, some are passed from person to person and even generationally, and some are based on irrationally bigoted thoughts. By themselves, attitudes can be limiting because they will often minimize the possibility of experience that an individual can have in any given situation or with any person.

Attitudes are generally classified as:

Positive
A generally upbeat and optimistic view of a person, situation, or even the world. This attitude set will drive confidence, hope, determination, sincerity, empathy, and serve to be magnetic with people. A positive expectation is a great example of a positive attitude. Consistent holding and projection of a positive attitude will draw other people of the same attitude qualities to you.

Negative
This set of thoughts drives a dim or pessimistic view of situations and people and can be very energy draining. This attitude type will also produce anger, doubt, frustration, and resignation from activities and people. Consistently possessing and projecting a negative attitude will draw others of the same to you and rebuff people with positive attitude qualities.

Neutral
This is neither a good nor a bad thing and it is also not a victory for us. Neutral is blah. There is no doubt but there is also no hope. Neutral attitudes often drive disconnection and disinterest. Nothing is either good or bad, it just is.

Sikken
A constant state of negativity combined with aggressiveness. This attitude will produce not only internal negativity but seek to dismantle the positive or neutral attitudes of all others. This attitude state must be avoided at all costs and can certainly produce some highly undesired behaviors.

So, to have a consistent set of positive, healthy, and connecting behaviors, we must always work to produce a positive attitude. Likewise, to maintain a changed behavior, we must manage our attitude that drives that behavioral change. Without that step, the behavior change will be short-lived.

A belief is a high level of trust and faith in something or someone. If you accept something as true now and, in the future, it becomes a belief. Our predictions of outcomes (i.e., "that will be great" or "that is really going to suck") is a belief. Connect that belief with an attitude and you have a powerful behavioral driver.

One of the most important steps we must take is to openly and assertively acknowledge that past events and interactions do not predict all future events and interactions. Just because someone treated you poorly yesterday does not mean they will treat you poorly today. Without this step, our history drive beliefs will produce a negative attitude that will drive very counterproductive behaviors.

Frequency and Intensity

Now before anyone goes sprinting towards the cliff in despair, or at the very least, second guessing all their behaviors and itemizing dozens of things that you must work on, please read this section. Maybe twice.

First, we have all limiting and self-defeating behaviors. All of us.

Secondly, but equally important, is that we will work on these in a programmatic and mostly linear method. We are not going to tackle ten poorly serving behaviors and six negative attitudes at one time. We are going to eat this elephant one bite at a time. These behaviors and attitudes were built in incremental steps and we are going to dismantle them the same way.

To secure a starting point and craft an action plan, we must gauge the severity and frequency of each. It is highly likely that you will find several limiting and self-defeating behaviors that impact your success and happiness. It is also likely, upon going through the list of them again, you will find many that creep in from time to time.

At the end of each behavior and attitude description is a brief scoring guide that is designed to help you understand the impact that each one has on your life and to triage where to begin to work on improvement. There is also a consolidated grid at the end of this book.

The scoring is simple and straightforward. The two criteria are frequency and estimated impact.

Frequency:

> Often – Does the behavior or attitude appear often or daily?

> Occasionally – Does the behavior or attitude show up periodically or infrequently?

> Never – You never display the behavior or attitude.

This will take some thought and reflection to see the true frequency that you display a particular attitude or behavior. We often tend to underestimate this, and this is a great area to seek some honest feedback from someone close to us. Their view may vary quite a bit from our own view but is more likely to be accurate than our self-view.

Estimated Impact:

> High – The behavior or attitude causes significant loss of opportunity, happiness, and success. You can look back and see how the behavior or attitude has had a big impact on your career, key relationships, or caused you anxiety and unneeded work.

Moderate – The attitude or behavior has caused you loss, but it was not severe. You regret the setback, yet it was not significant.

Low – The consequences of the behavior or attitude have had very little impact or effect on you.

Looking at impact forces us to examine the cost of our actions and poorly managed attitudes. This is not particularly pleasant and often will dredge up some painful memory points. This analysis is not designed to send you to regression therapy. It is important to clearly see the impact of these behaviors and attitudes and use this data to avoid future loss situations.

Your Style and Self-Defeating Behaviors

We are all very unique human beings and each of us brings our own style and approach to every situation and every interaction. And thank goodness. Our differences make life and work interesting. Likewise, we all have certain tendencies and propensities related to self-defeating and self-sabotaging behaviors as well.

For our purposes here, we will look through the lens of the DiSC behavioral assessment. The DiSC model is based on Marston's Model of Behavior and has both a high degree of validity and high degree of use. Over 35 million people have used and experienced the DiSC assessment.

DiSC is an acronym that stands for:

D – Dominance
i – Influence
S – Steadiness
C – Conscientiousness

Within this framework, each style has some predominant characteristics including:

D – Dominance
       Direct
       Fast Paced
       Assertive
       Results Oriented

i – Influence
       Social
       Upbeat and Enthusiastic
       People-Focused
       Animated and High-Spirited

S – Steadiness
       Calm
       Humble
       Accommodating
       Tactful and Thoughtful

Conscientiousness
       Accurate
       Analytical
       Private and Reserved
       Systemic

Every person has a primary driving style, and many have the influence of a secondary style. That secondary style often provides as much guidance as the primary style. For example, someone with a Dominance and Influence style can carry as many characteristics of the second style as the primary one.

For more information about the DiSC assessment, including how to acquire one and guides to better understand your results, please see the Reference section in this book.

As all of these primary driving styles communicate, make decisions, work in groups, lead, and behave differently, so too, do they have tendencies for self-defeating and self-sabotaging behaviors. We will include tendencies for each style at the end of each self-defeating behavior section to provide you with some general guidance based on your behavioral style. These are not absolutes, but rather general tendencies. If you have doubts about the tendencies for your style, seek feedback about those tendencies from a trusted source.

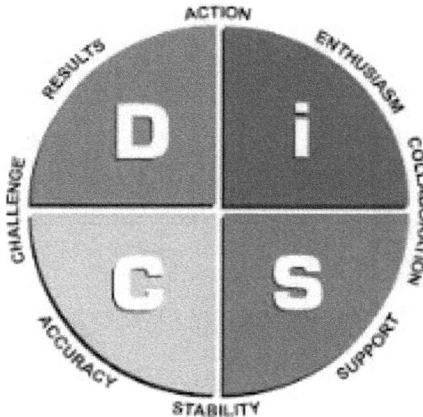

Impact of One

One of the easy temptations of reviewing self-limiting and self-defeating behaviors and associated beliefs and attitudes is to dismiss them quickly because they don't happen much.

I had the opportunity to recently talk with a long-term customer and friend about some feedback he received about his facial expressions. He had received some feedback from one of his team members that his facial expression made him unapproachable.

But this was just from one team member out of a large group that he leads. Not significant and easy to dismiss. Not worth even a second thought.

Or is it?

First, for every piece of evidence that you are aware of, there are many more in which you are not aware. Simply meaning that for everyone that brings something to your attention, there are at least two or three more that have noticed it but chosen to not say anything. Maybe because your facial expressions made you appear unapproachable.

And if it impacts one person, is it worth the effort to change or modify the behavior? In all relationships and leadership roles the answer must be yes. If it becomes a potential disconnect with one other person, it will become limiting or defeating to you. The impact on one person is certainly worth a little extra reflection and thought.

Self-Defeating Behaviors

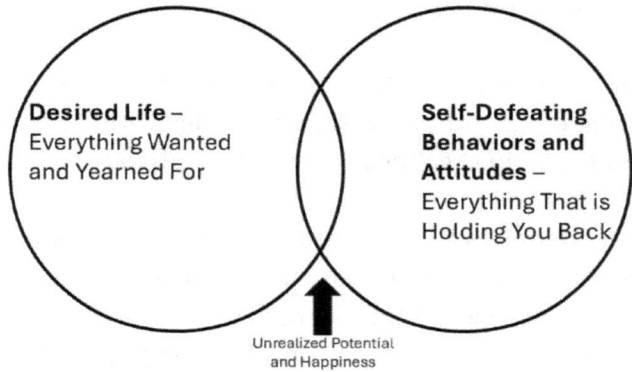

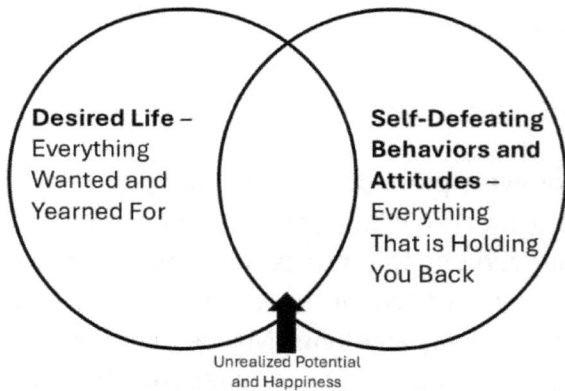

Desired Life –
Everything Wanted
and Yearned For

**Self-Defeating
Behaviors and
Attitudes –**
Everything That is
Holding You Back

Unrealized Potential
and Happiness

Little Impact from Self-Defeating Behaviors

Self-Defeating Behaviors

Desired Life –
Everything
Wanted and
Yearned For

**Self-Defeating
Behaviors and
Attitudes –**
Everything
That is Holding
You Back

Unrealized Potential
and Happiness

Moderate and Most Common Impact from Self-Defeating Behaviors

Self-Defeating Behaviors

Desired Life –
Everything
Wanted and
Yearned For

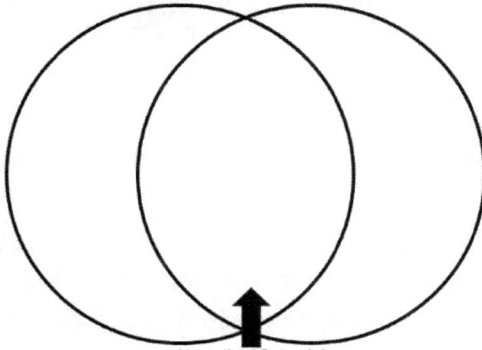

**Self-Defeating
Behaviors and
Attitudes –**
Everything
That is Holding
You Back

Unrealized Potential
and Happiness

High Impact from Self-Defeating Behaviors

Final Opening Thoughts and Encouragement

As with all human behavior changes, these movements will take time. Some will take a lot of time. Allow that and be gentle on yourself during the journey to changing yourself.

You will have setbacks. You will use some old, self-limiting habits, and you will scold yourself. Be as kind to yourself as you would to anyone else who is actively working on themselves. The setbacks are part of the process and improvement. Learn, try, succeed, fail, succeed again, fail less often. That is the adult human learning cycle.

Section II - The Limiting and Self-Defeating Behaviors

We will begin with a view of the limiting and defeating behaviors that most of us carry around. These are presented in order of the prevalence in which we have witnessed and recorded them in coaching and training sessions.

With each self-limiting and self-defeating behavior, a brief action plan will follow to help you navigate out of that pattern. Like with all our behaviors, these are choices, and we can be changing them today.

Please consider a couple of encouragements as you enter this section. First, keep an open mind and do not be so anxious to dismiss a behavior because you are sure you do not do, or you do not particularly like the description provided. Think about it a bit and see if you may creep into that behavior, even if only occasionally.

Secondly, and in the support of the first encouragement, please read this section, or at least skim it, twice. That will assist you in opening the possibility of limiting or defeating behavior and give you some time to think about situations in which it may have come out.

The behaviors we will be working on are:
Overthinking
Perfectionism
Impulsivity
Procrastination
People Pleasing / Overly Accommodating
Lack of People Skills
Need to be Right / Need to Win
Bottlenecking
Failure to Appreciate
Not Seeking or Accepting Feedback
Being Extra
Avoidance of the Difficult / Unpleasant
Wasting Time

Overthinking

"The primary cause of unhappiness is never the situation but your thoughts about it."
Eckhart Tolle

Never play Uno or Yahtzee with an overthinker.

This is the most common of the limiting and defeating behaviors and is most often responsible for missed opportunities in every segment of life. Overthinkers will craft stories about people, situations, and events in their own head.

Just a day ago, I fretted endlessly about asking a friend to coffee. What if she says no? What if she misreads my intention? What if she doesn't like coffee? Wasted a good 45 minutes of my life overthinking something with no risk. We're having coffee this coming Thursday. Similarly, I have offered a great little business opportunity to three of the Aegis Learning team members early this week. After two days, none of them have responded to this nominal risk and high-return potential chance.

Overthinking is the dwelling on and, often returning to thinking about the same thing. It is also a playing of "what ifs" that are focused on negative consequences and rarely about the positive potential of a situation or stimuli. Overthinkers will also devote undue amounts of time thinking about small and inconsequential issues and do not differentiate between a big thing and a little thing. To them all issues are worthy of the same degree of thought and analysis.

Those "What ifs" Have Low Probability and are a Figment of Your Imagination

The overthinker will add layers upon layers to even the most situations. They will create a root-looking network of thoughts usually wrapped around a series of "what ifs" or "what about that". They will also summon long-gone historical events to help justify their overthinking.

When unchecked and unmanaged, overthinking can lead to significant paralysis in action and loss of opportunity. In leadership and entrepreneurial roles this can be devastating. An overthinking leader or manager will drive his or her team absolutely nuts by sitting on the most fundamental and straightforward decisions. To anyone who leads, you must remind yourself that delay caused by overthinking risks your credibility just as the sand falls from the hourglass. Each grain of sand is your leadership credibility falling away with your delay.

Overthinkers will also tend to over-gather information and data about a particular issue or subject. Way more data than is reasonably needed. Many times, data gathering creates more "what ifs" and is truly not helpful.

The classic overthinker also processes thoughts about timing. They will look for and seek the "perfect" time. That time does not exist, and it will never exist. The result of this delay will be lost opportunity. Overthinkers will also avoid seeking out their needs such as asking for a raise, requesting consideration for a promotion, or asking someone out for a social occasion.

As a behavior, overthinking can be caused by risk avoidance, anxiety, and even depression. In a working environment, it can also be caused by a lack of feedback for good decisions combined with hyper-scrutiny when an error occurs.

The evil twin of overthinking is underthinking. Underthinking is the process of committing no thought to an issue or stimulus and making a rash and arbitrary decision. This is also not a desired course of action as all decisions, with the exceptions of using the restroom, trying the ice cream, and stopping at the red light should have some thought. If you are an overthinker, underthinking is not your target.

Overthinkers should always examine some driving attitudes as well as attacking the behavior itself. It is highly likely that several of the attitudes and beliefs in Section 3 will resonate with the classic overthinkers and need to have some time an attention.

To cure the overthinking behavior, begin to do the following:

1. Deadlines
Add deadlines to all your decisions and choices. Set a date and time when you will decide and make sure that deadline aligns with the needs of others. It makes no sense to set a deadline of tomorrow to decide on the dinner location tonight. This discipline of internal deadlines will be very helpful,

and you may have to write them down or add them to your task list as a reminder.

2. Proportionality and Scope

Another important strategy for overthinkers is the ability to ascertain the difference between a ten-cent problem and a million-dollar issue. As indicated earlier, overthinkers will often put the same thought and analysis into both. Save your superpower analysis for the big issues and let go of or ignore the inconsequential. This will take significant discipline from the overthinker and a very purposeful and mindful approach to identify issues as either important or unimportant. The key mantra of overthinkers is that everything is important and that must be rewired and removed from conscious thought.

3. Limit the Analysis Paralysis

Set a self-imposed limit of the number of "what if" scenarios that you will consider, process, and analyze. A great starting point would be three of them. After you have thought through those, it is time to decide and move. Tell yourself the scenarios you are crafting have no rooting in any reality or probability.

4. Apply Some Probability

Many of the "what ifs" that overthinkers process and lose time with have as much chance of occurring as you purchasing a nice blue raspberry snow cone in the depth of Hades. We have all heard those queries, usually near the end of a meeting, from an overthinker that starts with "have you thought about" followed by the extremely remote event that only the overthinker could imagine. As you think about a "what if" and determine the genuine likelihood of it occurring. Has it happened to you before? Does it happen often? What would have to come together to make it happen? Will Halley's Comet return prior to this "what if" happening? If the likelihood or probability of occurrence is less than 40% in a reasonable period, move on and make the choice now.

5. Benefits of Action Shift

Using a very purposeful approach, shift your thinking from what could go wrong to the benefits or results of the thought upon action. Focus on the benefits, value, and internal satisfaction points that would be generated from a decision or action. Look for the good and not the "what ifs".

6. Limit Input

A common behavior among overthinkers is to solicit input from others, often many other people. This "shopping for an answer" is designed to minimize the believed risk and validate the "what ifs" discovered by the overthinker. Limit your input to one or two trusted and honest people that will give you a true perspective of the issue and not just what you want to hear.

7. Now is the Perfect Time
The use of a self-imposed and assertively
uncomfortable deadline will cure a bit part of this,
but it is also necessary to make a shift in mindset.
Openly acknowledge that there is no such thing as
the perfect time, there is only time and the now.
This strategy will reappear a bit later.

Overthinking Frequency:
        Often   _____
        Occasionally   _____
        Never   _____

Overthinking Impact:

        High   _____
        Moderate   _____
        Low   _____

Behavioral High Tendency: Conscientiousness (C), Steadiness
(S) (Occasionally)
Behavioral Low Tendency: Dominance (D), Influence (i)

Perfectionism

"Perfect is the enemy of good."
Voltaire

Almost as pervasive and frequently seen as overthinking, perfectionism can have severely limiting, if not completely defeating, consequences.

Perfectionism is the pursuit of perfection, and sadly, perfect does not exist in anything touched by mere mortals. To a perfectionist, perfection is attainable with more work, more effort, more time, and just one more look at it.

The pursuit of and delivery of quality is noble and all of us should work to produce quality outcomes, interactions, services, and products. There is no real substitute for quality and quality should be a standard and not a goal. But quality is not without flaws. Perfectionism is the pursuit of a quality without flaws, a totally seamless experience, or the fairytale relationship.

The greatest impact of perfectionism is lost opportunity. When good, or even great, would have carried the day, the wasted time trying to be perfect loses out on the opportunity. That could come in the form of a sale, a hiring decision, or going out to dinner. Perfectionists also are very self-critical when it comes to their own perfection, or lack thereof. This can create significant consequences for needed confidence and self-esteem. Perfectionists also alienate the people around them because others believe they can never meet the standards of a perfectionist.

Perfectionists can also come across as aloof or arrogant to others. This stems from their judging of other people, situations, and places as not being perfect. The mind of the perfectionist creates a standard and nothing, and no one will live up to that standard. Smug they are (Yoda voice engaged). When the flaw-door is opened, the perfectionist will nitpick additional shortcomings and never provide an opening for escape. Everything is wrong at that point, and you will never be free of their scrutiny.

Perfectionists also create strains in important relationships. Because they hold others to high, and often unrealistic standards, they are constantly scrutinizing the behaviors of those close to them. When there are hiccups, or points of failure, they will abandon relationships and continue to seek someone who fulfills those unrealistic expectations. Simply put, the high expectations established by a perfectionist will have them driving many away from them, including their own families. Furthermore, this can create a lot of unresolved and unforgiven baggage in any relationship.

Judge Others Based on Their Ability, Not Your Unreachable Standards

We have a customer that we have worked with extensively, (training, coaching, and some consulting) that produces the most stunning customized homes. They are eye-popping and the designs are groundbreaking, never-before-seen products. Words alone could never do their homes justice. Their good house is an amazing dream home with unparalleled design and impeccable construction. When they meet their design standards, their customers drop their jaws. But the perfectionism rub comes in that some of their design team spends extra time shooting for absolute perfection. On the surface this sounds noble but with each delayed design is delayed construction and delayed closing of the home sale. There is no regard for the commercial reasonableness in this pursuit of perfection and the extra time taken has diminishing returns to the company. Their good is awesome but the pursuit of perfection creates unnecessary delays and costs.

Another customer who is a Chief Financial Officer struggles with some members of her team that will use dozens of hours reconciling accounts with discrepancies under a dollar. They want it to be perfect but fail to see the unreasonableness of the additional expenditure in time chasing perfection.

One other characteristic of perfectionists is the failure to accept mistakes or issues from others. When they see a typo in an email, they stop reading it. They completely dismiss a body of work because of a mistake or two. They assume that everything should have the perfection that they seek to provide.

On the personal side, perfectionists create incredibly high standards and expectations for everyone around them. From there, they become extremely judgmental to anyone not meeting those standards.

This also leads perfectionists to provide something called selective compassion or selective empathy. This phenomenon shows up both professionally and at work and can be devastating to relationships, especially when at the receiving end.

Consider this in relation to selective compassion:

> Maylin holds her life partner to a very high level of expectations. She also holds herself to similar standards. When Jason, her partner, has a point of failure, she quickly points it out, demands accountability for it, and locks it into her eternal memory, often bringing it up again.
>
> The same behaviors, and sometime even worse, are displayed by her father and she exercises no concern for them, even excusing them away. She grants her father grace and immediate forgiveness, while not giving Jason the same latitude.
>
> This lack of parity in expectations, standards, and accountability will cause harm in Maylin's relationship with Jason. Jason is certainly not blind and sees this selective compassion.

Similarly at work, selective compassion can look like:

> Suzy's favorite team member consistently provides high-quality work and meets the deadlines prescribed. Thomas is the ideal fit for the perfectionist sensibilities of Suzy. Some would consider Thomas her favorite and they seem to have a nice rapport.

Thomas recently went through several personal issues and missed a few deadlines and some of his quality slipped a bit. Suzy was gracious with Thomas and not only granted him forgiveness but also offered assistance to get him through the difficult time.

Kristin has had similar personal challenges in her life but has not really ever been Suzy's pal or even an insider within the department. Her priorities are different than Suzy's, but her work is still solid. When Kristin misses a deadline or has a minor lapse of quality, Suzy is all over her with coaching and accountability discussions.

Kristin certainly sees the difference in treatment and Suzy is risking creating a workplace dominated by favoritism or even a hostile working environment.

In any leadership role, working for a perfectionist is highly distressing for team members. Perfectionist leaders do not acknowledge the company standard for any product or deliverable, rather they utilize how well they would do something as the standard. They will withhold praise and appreciation until someone produces the same quality, or perfection, that they would, even on items that really add no material value (think font size, column width, color scheme). This grossly unfair approach to leadership will destroy the morale in any team and make that leader despised for perfectionism.

Perfectionists also like to "add value". This is a phrase that Marshall Goldsmith uses in his previously acknowledged work "What Got You Here Will Not Get You There". Dr. Goldsmith describes a scenario where someone provides an idea, and the other person suggests minor changes and edits that really don't impact the quality of the idea. They added value for no reason but their own ego and sense of their need to achieve perfection. He goes on to identify the impact this has on the person with the idea and their desire to ever present an idea again (which is greatly diminished or eliminated).

That same scenario plays out with perfectionists all the time, at home, at work, in social settings. The perfectionist cannot leave a great idea alone without the interjection of added value designed to make it perfect. Unfortunately, what the perfectionist does not understand is the alienation of relationships and disenfranchising of others that this causes.

To cure the perfection behavior, begin to do the following:

1. Reconcile to the Good
This is the most important step for perfectionists to embrace and challenge themselves. Realizing that good or great quality, especially if that is defined by your organization, is exactly the stopping point. No additional work is needed from you or others.

2. Diminishing Returns
The perfectionist must also recognize the costs and diminishing returns associated with continuing beyond good or great while pursuing perfection. Does it make sense to spend ten additional hours working on a good spreadsheet when the total value of the additional effort is nominal or only stylistic? Does it make sense to work on very good

designs for an extra fifty hours when the pricing or overall value proposition does not change?

3.   Reducing Judgement

Humans are judgmental creatures by our very DNA and composition. Perfectionists have perfected judgementalism and are constantly judging situations and people compared to their standard and vision of perfect. Not only is this grossly unfair but it is unhealthy when it becomes continuous. This action must be taken mindfully and purposefully with a solid intention to reduce negative judgements and to be more generous and appreciative.

4.   Say Thank You, And Nothing Else

Actively practice just saying the simple, and sincere, "thank you" when someone provides you something. Don't criticize, don't add value to it, don't even think about how you could have done it better. Just say "thank you".

This is about acceptance of work and efforts from people where they are. They are where they are and not where you think they should be. This is not about accepting substandard or poor quality in any way, shape, or form, but it is about acknowledging the good when it meets the needed standard, not your personal standard.

Thank you.

5. Reduce Criticality

Openly and mindfully look for the good in situations, people, and work product. Stop instantly seeing the room for improvement or the flaws. Actively practice seeking out the good that others do and the imperfect good that exists all around us. Note these and keep a journal of those items compared to how many times you see something wrong or something that could be done better. In about ten days you will find the notations and observations of the good taking a more prevalent and dominant role compared to the criticality.

Another target of your criticality is you. As a perfectionist you demand perfection from others and yourself. Reducing criticality needs to start and end with how hard you are on yourself. You are a perfect creation exactly as you are, flaws and all. Be more accepting and gentler with yourself especially when you have made a mistake (gasp) or did not deliver something with perfect quality. Take it easy on yourself and give yourself grace.

6. Perfect Does Not Exist

The perfect job, boss, team member, peer, neighbor, spouse, significant other, or parent doesn't exist. Humans have warts. People make mistakes. People say and do stupid stuff. Situations and events are not going to always go as planned or as desired. People sometimes react in emotional states. People have flaws and quirks that do not fit your nifty mold of a perfect person.

Craft your expectations in reality and not some fantasy you created. Create expectations built on satisfaction, happiness, and good, not perfection.

7. Forgive

As situations and people do not meet your expectations for perfection, intentionally practice forgiveness quickly. The great misconception about forgiveness is that it requires forgetting what happened and that is simply not true. Forgiveness is the solemn commitment and promise that whatever occurred or whoever wronged you or did not meet your expectations will not influence future interactions with them. It also does not mean that accountability is lost, it simply means that you are releasing the strain of letting whatever happened not impact you further. Forgiveness is one of the healthiest and most important practices for your own personal emotional condition and in protecting the relationships we have.

Perfectionism Frequency:
    Often   _____
    Occasionally   _____
    Never   _____

Perfectionism Impact:

    High   _____
    Moderate   _____
    Low   _____

Behavioral High Tendency: Conscientiousness (C)
Behavioral Low Tendency: Dominance (D), Influence (i),
Steadiness (S)

Impulsivity

"There is perhaps no psychological skill more fundamental than resisting impulse."
Daniel Goleman

Impulsivity is the diametric opposite of procrastination. Impulsivity is the overly quick reaction, often done with no thought of consequence or risk, to any situation or stimuli. It is often driven by an inflated emotional state such as anger, fear, jealousy, or even love. Impulsive actions, when done continuously or constantly, will destroy a career or relationship.

Overly impulsive also shows up in desires for immediate resolution. It is that belief, which drives impulsive behaviors, that everything must be done and fixed now. No time to think, just do it. No analysis needed, just talk or work through it now. This false-prioritization and false-urgency is very common in a lot of people. It happened ten minutes ago so it must be resolved now. This will often create false fixes that may temporarily bandage some of the issues or create a situation where you can claim a "win", but they do little for any long-term resolution and frequently stir resentments or half-hearted compromises. This self-defeating behavior also shows itself with impatience when receiving a response to a text, email, or return call. Impulsivity needs an immediate response and can't stand the delay.

Striking a balance between being decisive, a highly desired characteristic, and being impulsive or rash, will be a challenge for many people. As discussed previously, we want to move and act. But we also need to do so in a thoughtful manner that examines risk and consequence.

Military snipers are trained to breathe, intentionally, and to focus, taking as much time as needed. They are dutiful in measuring range, wind, and terrain before responding to a target. There are distinct reasons why first responders like firefighters and police walk to a critical situation. They do not run. That is to simply control their emotions and adrenaline that often comes with these types of events. We have the capacity, if used intentionally, to respond to events and situations with that same required discipline.

Now when the fire bell rings, I want you to be impulsively decisive. When a crisis occurs, I want you to respond based on your knowledge and impulses for safety and helpfulness. But outside of critical situations, impulsiveness is highly self-defeating. Similarly, adding spontaneity to life will add a high degree of richness. Spontaneity is something you consider. It has thought into what your current situation is and what you have planned. It considers possible consequences, in an instant rather than a long drawn out thought process. It is the view of your calendar and task list and deciding quickly that a day at the beach is what is needed.

Impulsive actions and behaviors can also be driven by assumptions. When we assume a certain situation is occurring or a person is doing something. These assumptions will drive an impulsive response based on limited or no evidence. This is also a sign of a significant lack of emotional control and self-management.

The behavioral opposite of impulsiveness is to be thoughtful, appropriately analytical, and tactful. Everyone wants to be around that person. Not many want to be around constantly impulsive souls.

Take Some Time and Consider the Consequences of Your Actions and Words

Impulsivity has the possibility of exposing us to huge, and untenable, risk factors, and causing great harm to relationships and the people around us. Many careers have been harmed without the ability to repair based on one impulsively spoken word or action. Sadder still is the harm to an important relationship because of one rash act or statement uttered in high emotion. One of the most common impacts of impulsivity is the loss of time needed to return to fix, or have others fix, the mistakes made while being rash. The false narrative that the complete box was checked, and checked quickly, often leads to silly mistakes and overlooked details.

There is also a very dark side of impulsive behavior too. Many people suffering from addictions, drug, gambling, alcohol, nicotine, and sex, struggle with reacting to and being impulsive when presented with opportunity or triggering stimuli. To wit: a person with an alcohol dependency would struggle to control impulses when confronted with a party serving alcohol. Impulse control then becomes critical to long-term recovery for addicts. Impulsivity will setback all addiction recovery.

Impulsivity can also mutate into revenge relatively easily or be used to demonstrate victimhood in some situations. When unregulated, impulsivity has extended and extensive consequences. The good news is that this behavior can be easily contained and almost eliminated in most people.

The root of being impulsive is found in the self-imposed, self-created need for immediate gratification. We need to show someone how smart we are. We need to demonstrate how clever and funny we can be. We need to win the situation. We need to show someone that we are right, and they are wrong. We need to make sure they know we are in charge, and we make the rules here. Within this cause, we see significant clues on how to change this behavior.

Understanding unintended consequences is an important element as we move into solving impulsivity. An unintended consequence is that action or set of actions that are sent into motion by your impulsive response. They are the responses you were not anticipating. They are the losses you did not realize could happen. They are the risks becoming reality that you did not analyze before acting or speaking. We cannot always see all unintended consequences, but we can certainly see more using time and space prior to acting out or reacting.

A common example from a working environment would be:

> Sandra stops into Pete's office right before break time and asks if she can leave early today to see her son's soccer game. She is caught up with her work and there are no role coverage issues. Without any thought, Pete, the caring manager, says "of course",

A day later, Sam makes his way to Pete's office to explain that his team is playing on Monday Night Football, and he would appreciate leaving early to secure his corner seat and the local tavern. He too, is caught up on all his work.

Unfortunately, Pete's impulsive response to Sandra, driven by his need to be seen as a good manager, has created a bit of a pickle. He realizes now that when he said yes to Sandra, he has to say yes to Sam or create a working environment where team member requests are not judged fairly, or team members are receiving preferential treatment. Unwittingly, Pete's impulse to be seen as a loveable manager has set precedence.

Another far too often occurring example from work is:

Andrew has received a customer complaint about Shelley. Being the responsive manager that he is, Andrew immediately, without any investigation, thought or analysis, goes down and barks at Shelley. He tells her in no uncertain terms that this is unacceptable, cannot occur again, and must be resolved immediately. Andrew does not bother seeking Shelley's side of the story.

Shelley is a long-term, highly engaged, team member that routinely interacts with dozens of customers each day. She has received nothing but high satisfaction ratings from those interactions and has even won awards from the company based on the service levels she provides.

The interaction with Andrew devastates Shelley. Over a very short period, her engagement drops, her service level falls, and she starts calling in sick much more frequently than ever before. She has also subscribed to several internet job search services and is actively looking to leave the job she once loved.

Great job Andrew! Your impulsiveness is about to cost you one of the best team members you have. Your need for immediate action and to extract a pound of flesh for some mistake is going to cost you far more than one unhappy customer. No perspective on the service volume Shelley handles. No view of how she has always been a great service provider. No grace in viewing the total value of Shelley. No, it was all about your urgency in resolving a situation that wasn't even a situation.

A final working example would be:

Pete sees the hotel check-in line beginning to form at an unusual time of day. Not wanting guests to wait, he immediately summons two front desk team members from their lunch break to take care of the forming backlog. This certainly seems noble and with a focus on customer service and taking care of the guests and business.

Unfortunately, Pete committed a blatant violation of his team member's protected labor law rights with his impulsive decision. It seemed like the right thing to do, but it has the potential of backfiring in a big way.

Now an example from life outside of work:

> Tom sees a Facebook post from Jim that stirs up some negative emotions, rubs him the wrong way, and simply pisses him off. He has created an internal narrative that he has been wronged and needs to respond immediately.
>
> Tom responds with a very snide comment. Not verbose but certainly makes his point. And rather than let it die there, he responds again to the person that offended him. And again. All providing Tom with the immediate gratification of being right and somehow being harmed by the original post.
>
> Jim unfriends Tom and vows to never speak to him again. Tom has exposed himself to some embarrassment and ridicule because of his impulsive need to be right. All because he chose to either ignore or respond in a more thoughtful manner.

To successfully improve impulsive behaviors, embrace:

1. Pause and Slow Down

Taking a pause prior to any response might be the best advice in this book. Take a few seconds, minutes, or hours, whatever you need to really think about the impact of your actions and words. This time can also be used to manage your emotional composition that drives so many rash and impulsive behaviors.

2.   Respond and Not React
Purposefully and mindfully become a deliberate
responder. This not only requires the above pause, but
it also requires intentional thinking about what you
want to say, how you want to say, and even the
necessity of any response.

3.   Look at Long-Term Consequences
Impulsivity is built around a need for immediate
satisfaction. The need to be funny. The need to be
right. The need to prove a point. Before you venture
down that path, take a look at the long-term
consequences of your actions. Will relationships be
harmed? Will your credibility be lost or damaged? Will
your reputation be harmed? Will you embarrass other
people?

4.   Look for Unintended Consequences
Although never perfect, take a few moments and try to
look at possibilities that you are not anticipating. You
may even choose to get some feedback from a trusted
source on this. Different eyes can often see
unintended consequences that we cannot see.

5.   Get Your Emotions in Check
Negative emotions are often a primary driver of
impulsive words and actions. Check your emotional
composition and determine what you are feeling. Take
some time to get those emotions regulated and back to
a neutral or positive state. Go for a walk. Listen to
some calming music. Journal your feelings. Exercise.

6. Find Longer Term and Personal Satisfaction
If we look closely, we can often channel the need for immediate satisfaction into looking for a longer-term point of satisfaction. You may not have proven that you were right today, but you preserved a key relationship that you will need to work on moving forward. This is easily expressed as being wrong to win, or to win ultimately. Not taking an opportunity to embarrass someone with your humor will keep them as a long-term encouraging supporter in the future.

We also can internalize our points of satisfaction. We can smile to ourselves when we are right or think of something funny without the need to share it with the world. Be careful and do not look smug when doing this.

7. Show Some Grace
Someone wrongs you or says something completely inappropriate to or about you. Your first, impulsive thought is to retaliate and immediately respond to this slight or perceived slight. This impulsive behavior never ends well and rarely ends any situation. Show some simple grace and let some things slide. If there was really no harm done or the harm was minimal or ego-based only, let it go. Grant some forgiveness and chalk it up to someone having a bad day or someone being thoughtless. Let it go.

Another side of showing grace is to not get too worked up over the impulsive behaviors of others. Just as we will need some forgiveness from time to time, we need to allow other people that same space. Do not be so quick to criticize the impulsivity of others when it is an exception in their behavior.

8. Examine Your Motives

Looking at our motives and motivations is healthy and helps us stay grounded and reminds us about our "why", our purpose. When faced with an opportunity for an impulsive behavior or word, examine why you are thinking about doing it. Often times this will yield some unattractive motivations such as proving a point, revenge, drawing attention to yourself, or embarrassing someone else. When you realize these are not appropriate motivations for any action, it is easy to let go of the impulsivity. Afterall, would you want someone to use those motivations on you?

9. Check Your Assumptions

Before taking rash action or speaking out of emotion, examine the assumptions you are making and the validity of the evidence supporting those assumptions. Are you crafting a narrative based only on your own thoughts? Are your emotions driving your assumptions? Is your own insecurity about something or someone making these assumptions seem real and reasonable?

10. Create Alternatives

If, like me, you remember telling your kids to count to ten when they are angry or upset, this little section will resonate with you. When you feel the need to have an impulsive action or speak rash words, create an alternative for yourself. That could be as simple as counting or a bit more elaborate like playing a quick game on your phone. Really anything will work if you are distracted from the impulsive behaviors. Some of the more common impulse alternatives include taking a walk, going to work out, calling someone, or immediately moving to a task. So, the next time you're tempted to stalk the ex's Facebook page, pull out your phone and play a much healthier game of solitaire. The next occurrence of wanting to lash out at a co-worker for a mistake she or he made, go for that walk around the building.

Impulsivity Frequency:
    Often   _____
    Occasionally   _____
    Never   _____

Impulsivity Impact:
    High   _____
    Moderate   _____
    Low   _____

Behavioral High Tendency: Dominance (D), Influence (i)
Behavioral Low Tendency: Conscientiousness (C), Steadiness (S)

Procrastination

"There comes a time when you have to stop revving up the car and shove it into gear."
David Mahoney

The accepted and classic definition for procrastination is delaying, postponing, or deferring something until later. Later is a word that the procrastinator uses a lot. Later, as in I'll finish reading this later.

Procrastination is closely related to perfectionism in that it causes missed opportunities both in a working environment and for us personally. The cost of procrastination is a missed opportunity. Consider the poor person who had great dreams and plans for the Pear Computer and associated operating system. It was an elegant dream with great design concepts and an even cooler logo (a pear with a bite out of the right side). But rather than jump and act, this soul sat around and worked on other things, overthought the process, and never really got going. Sad, and certainly exaggerated, but it occurs every day.

The classic procrastinator uses a variety of self-created excuses for continued procrastination. The most often cited excuse is a lack of time. This hollow excuse is really about a lack of prioritization (see below) and a lack of commitment to do what is needed.

When faced with a deadline, the procrastinator pushes the envelope all the way to the point of being late and often rushes the deliverable. Quality suffers, and thought is non-existent in this kind of waiting followed by frantic chaos. Without a deadline, the procrastinator will kick something down the road indefinitely until the point the task or project no longer has value.

The busy addiction often afflicts the classic procrastinator. To look at them, they appear to be busy, in some cases overwhelmed by stuff, but there is no regard for what they are busy at. It is not nearly enough to be busy or even really busy, but you must know what the targets and priorities are.

As You Are Delaying, Someone Else is Seizing an Opportunity

As much as the procrastinator misses opportunities in a working environment, they also miss out in their personal lives as well. Failure to respond to invitations lead to unavailable reservations for dinner. Non-responsiveness leads to future invitations not being extended.

Some causative factors that make people procrastinators include an intolerance for any degree of risk, lack of any type of organizational and time management skills, the inability to distinguish priorities, and a1 fear of being first (yes, that is a real thing and it's why some people can never be on time to a party or meeting). Sometimes procrastinators come from a long line of procrastinators passing this defeating behavior from generation to generation.

To eliminate procrastination, begin (as in now, not next week) to do the following:

1. Set and Adhere to Deadlines
Please refer to the Overthinking Section for more on creating and working with deadlines.

The only additional consideration for procrastinators to is move deadlines forward from the actual deadline. So, if the report is due on Friday, create and document a Wednesday deadline for yourself. If your friend needs to hear about the dinner plans by Monday, create and document a Saturday (the prior one, not the later one) deadline.

2. Create Increments
Because we often work with large tasks and projects, it is often necessary, and extremely helpful for procrastinators, to break them down into smaller incremental pieces. If budget projections are due at the end of the month, break each category like income, payroll, fixed expenses, variable expenses, and miscellaneous items into individual tasks and spread them out weekly. At the end of the month, the sum of the incremental tasks is the budget is done and on time.

Likewise, if you need to clean the garage by the end of the month, separate the elements out like yard equipment, tools, storage items, and attack each category weekly or daily until the garage is clean. Eat the elephant one bite at a time.

3. Create Priorities

Procrastinators must learn to devote their time and energy to where it has the highest impact and importance. The first step in creating and adhering to a priority-based system is to inventory what you must do, what you have going on. Often a procrastinator will use a last-in, first-out methodology in dealing with tasks and projects. So, no matter how important or unimportant something is, if it is the first on the stack (or top of the email inbox), it gets the attention. This approach is fatally flawed and will continue with the cycle of missed opportunities.

We always advocate for a simple, but elegant, prioritization system. After you have identified everything you need to do, assign a priority of either one, two, or three. Anything much more complicated than this will end up being more bother than utility. Priority one should be if it impacts a customer or makes or saves money. Priority two is if it is a team member's need or issue and finally, priority three is anything else of organizational value.

From a personal perspective, priority one would be if it is for your spouse, significant other, or kids. Priority two would be for another family member or friend and priority three would be the general good of the household.

This priority system begs a question about what is not a one, two, or three. This will test both the procrastinators and the perfectionists. So, if it is not categorized as a priority, the short answer is it should get none of your time and attention and should be removed from any inbox or task list. That's right. Gone. Bye. Kaput. For leaders, they will always have the option of delegating these types of things to others but that should only be done after analysis of legitimate value to someone or the organization. For everyone else, we need to let go and consciously note that we have no regret or second thought about doing them.

Another challenge of a priority system is what to do with those things we like to do but are not high priorities or no priority at all. I enjoy mowing the yard but comparing that to other priorities, it is meaningless especially when I have the option of outsourcing that chore. Simply said, if it is no priority, you have no business devoting time to it, even if you like it.

One, two, three, or no priority and no action. That simple.

The final part of using a prioritization system is using it. That means devoting the plurality of your time and energy to the high priorities (ones) while taking care of the twos and threes as time allows and never in conflict with a higher priority. Never.

4. Develop Risk Tolerance

A shared characteristic of perfectionists and procrastinators is a lack of risk tolerance. This must be developed if you are going to leave the self-defeat of procrastination.

Every day when you hop on the freeway, you are taking a risk. You risk the behavior and consideration of other drivers. You risk the design quality of the road engineers. You risk a lot. There are those people that are paralyzed by this proposition but most of us are willing jump into our cars and make the needed trek.

What separates this risk from others that we face at work or home is the degree of scrutiny from others. When we push a decision or act quickly, we risk the critique from others. When we procrastinate the same decision or action, some of that is mitigated. For people who share overthinking and procrastination, this phenomenon is especially true.

Use a simple little bit of math to help yourself with risk tolerance. Look at what the real chances are of a negative event. And please note that on unknow events, the chances are exactly equal of a positive outcome and a negative outcome.

5. Time and Task Planning

One of the reasons that procrastinators procrastinate or proclaim failure with all tries to stop procrastination is that they have poor time management skills and practices.

To reduce procrastination, you must balance your "to dos" with the available time that you have and avoid dumping everything going on into one giant task list. Consider listing seven tasks needed today and your calendar is packed from the start of the day to the end of the day. You have no chance of accomplishing those and it is discouraging folly to even list them for the day.

A more thoughtful approach and one with a significantly higher chance of success is to spread your tasks out based on available capacity. Look at your calendar and see where you have the capacity and map out your tasks where the time allows. Also avoid a master task list (or honey-do list) at all costs. These can become discouraging based on the sheer volume of items and so overwhelming to the procrastinator that nothing gets done or even started.

6. Prioritize the Unpleasant
One of the most frequently procrastinated items are those things that are unpleasant or that we don't want to do. Ugly stuff. That difficult conversation. Reconciling the account that you've ignored for three years. Cleaning the hall closet. Whatever your unpleasant is, make it an early priority during the day, absolutely first thing. Using this approach, you are devoting the highest energy you have to a difficult or undesired task and thus getting it done quicker but the greatest benefit is in

that it will be out of the way early and pave the way for a great rest of the day.

7.   Use the 25 – 5 Rule
This may be more of a productivity enhancer, but it will help procrastinators break up larger projects that they are delaying or otherwise ignoring. Work on a task or project for 25 minutes, take five minutes off to clear your mind, get fresh coffee or whatever. Then shift to another task or project for 25 minutes with the five-minute break repeated and then move back to the first project and repeat until completed. This keeps your mind fresh and gives you a break to avoid the diminishing returns of trying to power through a four-hour project or task. Give this a try and you will be amazed at the spike in productivity and the loss of drag from working on one thing for a long period of time.

Please note that in some cases, procrastination can be caused by underlying psychological problems such as depression or anxiety. If you believe that may be the case, please contact a counselor or therapy professional.

Procrastination Frequency:
    Often   _____
    Occasionally   _____
    Never   _____

Procrastination Impact:

    High   _____
    Moderate   _____
    Low   _____

Behavioral High Tendency: Conscientiousness (C), Steadiness (S)
Behavioral Low Tendency: Dominance (D), Influence (i)

People Pleasing / Overly Accommodating

"Care about what other people think and you will always be their prisoner."
Lao Tzu

People pleasing and being overly accommodating is a severe type of self-defeating behavior. This one is not just limiting but it can absolutely cause you, your career, and the people around you harm.

On the surface, people pleasing and accommodating sound great and certainly some people could use some more of it in their lives. Maybe just a little accommodating or pleasing to others. And certainly, I do not want any of you to become obstinate, objecting, difficult asses because of this. Quite the contrary, I want you to be a good person, but without sacrificing your own needs and happiness. That's what happens to people pleasers and the overly accommodating. They sacrifice their own needs, emotional health, and boundaries to make others happy and ignore their own happiness and well-being.

People pleasers struggle with any form of the word "no". It just gets stuck in their throat even when they know the answer should be a hard "no". They agree to just about anything reasonable and will offer help even when they do not have the capacity for any of it. They rarely turn down any request and many times this creates an undue burden on their time and capacity. They will work incredibly hard not to disappoint anyone to whom they have made a commitment to help. People pleasers often report feeling a sense of great burden to take care of the needs of everyone around them, work and at home. They often create obligations to help others where no such obligation exists.

Another sign of people pleasing includes an inability to disagree unless in extremely subtle ways and many times, not at all. People pleasers will concede in conversations even about a subject they are passionate about just to not upset the other person. They can morph from liberal Democrat to conservative Republican based on who they are talking with and the subject at hand. In extreme cases, people pleasers and over-accommodating people take on the personality traits of those that they are around. They chameleon whoever they are around and validate everything that comes out of other people's mouths, demonstrating an agreement and alignment with that person. In general, people pleasers and over-accommodators will be conflict adverse or conflict avoidant and they will struggle to ask about anything that resembles their own interest. A healthy working environment and a healthy home has conflict that is rooted in issues, managed without emotion, and dealt with in real time. Avoiding conflict does not resolve it but makes it worse later when it has no choice but to boil to the surface.

Avoiding any form of even the most benign conflict and being extremely uncomfortable or upset when someone is mad at you is also a signal that you are a people pleaser. The overly accommodating and people pleasers are very uncomfortable in these types of situations and will then bend their own needs and desires even further to restore peace.

People pleasers also struggle with self-care as all their energy is directed to the needs of others. They will never prioritize taking time to care for themselves when there are unmet needs, or perceived unmet needs of others that they believe they need to fulfill first. This can often lead to a significant overwhelming feeling, resentment, and frustration for the people pleaser. The motivation to change is often a breakdown or shock-type event that makes them realize they can't fill the cup of others when their glass is empty.

You Must Take Care of Yourself Prior to Caring for Other People

People pleasing or the desire to please everyone can also morph into a quest for being popular. The people pleaser wants everyone to think highly of them and they manage their image and projections accordingly. Unfortunately, this leads to an avoidance of difficult decisions and contributes to failing to confront challenging conversations. The people pleaser will avoid any decision or discussion that jeopardizes their popularity with others or threatens how others may view them.

One final symptom of people pleasing is overly validating and overly apologizing. People pleasers will often go out of their way to validate the thoughts, words, and feelings of others, including many times when this is not needed. They can even end up taking on the emotions and feelings of others as well.

And equally often they will use leading apologies or apologize for their actions when none is needed. Consider this example:

> Steve approaches his leader to talk about a manager opening in the department. Because he is a people pleaser and his boss is a busy woman, Steve starts by saying "Sandy, I'm sorry to bother you but I would like to talk about upcoming manager position".

Or another example from a home setting:

> Shannon has been avoiding talking about her needs with her husband for a long time but has finally worked up the courage to do so. She leads by saying "I'm sorry for bringing this up but...". She later apologizes again for starting a small conflict.

One key strategy for people-pleasers is to develop alternatives to apologizing to lead a conversation. Consider this approach for Steve and Shannon:

> Can we please talk about the situation that occurred last night with our friends?

> May we please talk about the manager opening in the department?

Both are meeting their needs in a direct way without being overly assertive and certainly not rude. Save the apologies for when it matters and when it will have some real value.

It is painfully obvious that the key penalty for people pleasing, and overly accommodating behavior is a complete disregard for your own needs. Your needs are not just second, they are non-existent in most interactions because you choose to always put the needs of others first. Noble sounding but extremely self-defeating.

Now some of you are going to raise a hand and object that this Mother Teresa-esque type of selflessness is noble and should be encouraged and certainly not discouraged. The needs of others are extremely important and must not be ignored, but we cannot run ourselves dry of emotional and physical energy helping others and not paying attention to our own needs. There also comes a point that when we are overlooking our own needs, we will withdraw and shut down. Your needs are every bit as important as everyone else's.

To move past people pleasing and over-accommodating, begin using the following tactics:

1. Buy Yourself Some Time
Because your automatic answer is always a yes, learn to add some time to your decisions and analyze if you can truly help or assist. Start saying something like "please let me have until the end of the day" or "I will let you know tomorrow morning" for you to be able to see if you can fit the needed time and effort into what you already have going on. You can use this time to check your calendar and task list to ensure that you truly have capacity for another project or volunteer for the event. This extra space also allows the requestor to reflect a bit on what they are asking for.

2. Use a No Substitute
You struggle with saying no but you can begin using some "no" substitutes. No lite, if you will. Try saying "I'm sorry I can't" or "Unfortunately, I just don't have the room for that right now" instead of a hard no. You will also want to develop a tolerance for saying no if someone continues to press or badger you for something that you just don't have the room for in your current schedule.

3. Create and Share Boundaries
Boundaries are those self-created fences that guard you. They protect your time, emotional energy, and overall capacity for something. We all operate within the boundaries of law and ethics and personal boundaries serve to help you help yourself.

First look at the people that often take advantage of your accommodating nature. Craft a limit for talking with and interacting with them. When they hit the limit, cut off the interactions for a time.

Next create a boundary for the number of things you take on during a week or month. These can be work projects, extra tasks, home projects, or volunteer work. When you hit the limit, stop taking on anything extra until your capacity catches up.

Now the hard part about boundaries. You can set them all you want but until you share them with others, they have absolutely no impact. So yes, you must tell your boss, wife, kids, sister, church friends, dog rescue peeps, whoever, that you have some boundaries and are not going to take on everything for everyone anymore. And be prepared to tell them why.

4.   Develop Tolerance for Conflict
People pleasers and over-accommodators must develop a small tolerance level for routine conflicts. This will require that you do some self-management to understand that conflicts are not bad, conflicts do not have to be emotionally charged, and most importantly, conflict is the root of all progress and growth. Without some conflict, or disagreement, we can never innovate or produce continuous improvement. Tell yourself that conflict is not only okay, but it is highly desirable, if it is managed at an issue or process level and the people in the conflict effectively manage their emotions during the conflict event.

To assist in the tolerance for conflict, note the objectives for any conflict or disagreement, set a time to discuss it, and stick to your talking points. Stay resilient and do not take the bait of a personalized or emotional response. Stick to your points and stay focused on the issue or process, not the person.

5.   Limit Apologies
Apologies are an awesome display of empathy and certainly have value when you have made an error, but people pleasers lead with an apology far too often. Catch and stop yourself when you are about to apologize for bringing up an issue or expressing your needs. Similarly, do not apologize for your opinions on a subject, even if they are contrary to the opinions of

others. And certainly, never apologize for needing or wanting to be heard.

6. Improve Relationship Depth
Growing your relationship depth with other people will make it significantly easier to say no or to ask for time to think about something before committing to it. As you get to know people more deeply you will feel more comfortable telling them your needs and articulating your boundaries. Conflict resolution also becomes easier when relationship depth is present.

7. It's Okay to be a Little Selfish
If it's important to you or you enjoy doing it, then do it without regard for the needs and desires of others. This will not work all the time but sometimes you need to do what is best for you and not the family, coworkers, boss, spouse, or any others. Don't be so anxious to give away your time with friends, yoga class, or other things of personal enjoyment and make this part of your boundary set. Take time and prioritize the time for your own self-care.

8. Stop Worrying About What Others Think
People pleasers often do so to curry favor with others. The people that you want in your life, personally and professionally, will like you for who you truly are and not what you do for them. The people that pretend to like you only when you do things for them are not the people you want or need in your life. Think twice, and maybe three times, about how much you worry about what others think about you and if those people really should matter to you. The loss or ill opinion of a

person or two that doesn't like you because you didn't subordinate everything else you have going on to do their favor, is worth it compared to a healthier and happier you. Be you, boundaries and no responses included, and the right people will stick with you.

9.   Challenge How You View Yourself
Closely related to worrying about what other people think about you, you need to challenge how you value yourself. Your value is not about how much you do for others nor is it how popular you are with others. Your value is deeper than that and not about what you do but rather about who you are, your core person. You are not tick marks on a task list, you are much more than that.

10. Make the Difficult Decisions
Rather than kicking the can down the road, face the difficult conversations and decisions directly and without regard to your popularity or standing with others. Aim for respect, not being universally loved.

People Pleasing / Over Accommodating Frequency:
    Often   _____
    Occasionally   _____
    Never   _____

People Pleasing / Over Accommodating Impact:
    High   _____
    Moderate   _____
    Low   _____

Behavioral High Tendency: Steadiness (S), Influence (i)
Behavioral Low Tendency: Dominance (D), Conscientiousness (C)

Lack of People Skills

"How you treat the one reveals how you regard the many, because everyone is ultimately a one."
Stephen Covey

The lack of meaningful people skills is certainly limiting and, in many cases, totally defeating for people. You don't have to be the life of the party, but you don't ever want to be the person that everyone avoids either. We occupy this blue marble with 7.89 billion other souls and the ability to interact with and get along with other people is paramount. People skills should also not be dependent on beer count, as everyone gets more charming by drink number two.

The defending argument for a lack of people skills always relies on self-identification as either shy or as an introvert. Introvert or not, naturally shy, or not, we all need a minimum baseline of people skills to operate in the working environment and in even small social circles. Shyness and being an introvert are hardwired parts of our personalities, while the use of people skills is a learned behavior that can be embraced by all.

Failure to utilize commonly used people skills will dramatically hamper workplace success and the ability to work effectively with others, regardless of your technical expertise. Rather than being a valued team member, you will be the person everyone avoids. If you desire to move into higher levels of leadership, your people skills become even more important and more magnified and valued by others.

The lack of good people skills is often a behavioral symptom of unhealed losses and unforgiven wrongs. The weight we carry with those things will destroy our energy to properly connect and interact with people. Likewise, negative expectations and hyper-rigidity will also negatively impact our ability to use great people-based skills.

Consider this workplace scenario with significant consequences:

> Shawn has been in the fire service for over 30 years and is a technical expert in the field. He is a walking encyclopedia of all things fire and what it means to be a first responder. The problem is that he is also an unapproachable, grumpy, curmudgeon who has not said good morning to anyone since 1994, and that was begrudging. He never asks about anyone and never seems interested in anything but his core work.
>
> Vicky is a relatively new fire officer with only five years of direct experience and has not yet seen it all in her industry, yet she is affable, approachable, asks about others, and demonstrates care for others. She has great people skills and is highly likeable.
>
> A captain's job is opening in the agency and both Shawn and Vicky will be applying. The panel interviewers will focus on the ability to lead the team and create meaningful connections with all the team. They are looking for someone who can rally the team

when needed and who will have a positive impact on the morale in the department.

Who gets this job is obvious and this scenario repeats itself hundreds of times a day. People skills are more valued in a highly performing workplace than technical skills.

People skills are also the foundation of relationships with others. I have encountered numerous people who are painfully hard to get to know because of their lack of people skills. Sure, once you get to know them, they are fine humans. Nevertheless, many people give up trying to get to know them because there is nothing there in the first two, three, or twenty interactions.

Another scenario to consider with a personal angle:

> Two people join a meetup group at the same time. Lawrence is outgoing and loves to greet and talk with people. He has quickly built a reputation as someone they love to have on hikes and group outings.

> Cindy goes to the events but doesn't talk to anyone and when she does it has the tone of someone having a wisdom tooth removed. People try to engage with her, but she provides one-word answers and nothing more.

As the group grows and breaks into several subgroups, who is going to get the ongoing invitations?

Even in a close interpersonal relationship like a marriage, a baseline of people skills is needed for ongoing happiness and relationship success. Relationships fail without a healthy flow of communication, doses of empathy, and a great deal of interest in the other person.

People skills are best defined as those interactions and engagements that serve to connect with people. Most are communication based, meaning that communication must flow well, and you must have some great communication skills. All require a level of discipline to turn them into a habit set. The core communication skill needed in people interaction is listening, real listening, not formulating your response, not letting your mind wander off, not interrupting, but real validated listening with the singular focus on the listening event and nothing else. As your listening skills improve, you'll be amazed how people begin to migrate to you and value time with you.

Next on the importance triage of communication skills is our tone, how we sound to others. Most people have very little understanding of their own tone and the impact it can have on our other people skills. Visualize two people saying the exact same words, something simple like "thank you", and a person with a harsh tone makes it sound almost punitive, while someone with a softer and more sincere tone makes the message much more believable and valuable. We craft this narrative about how we sound (our tone), and that narrative is completely removed from reality. How many of you have listened to a recording of your own voice? Did you enjoy what you heard? Unless you are a trained voice actor, singer, or just particularly fond of yourself, you probably didn't enjoy that experience. Solicit some feedback about your tone from some trusted sources and then begin to manage it by doing a few voice exercises for inflection (no one likes monotone) and learning to lower or raise your assertiveness as needed in any conversation.

The final couple of points related to communication involve clarity and richness. Clarity is about delivering messages in a way they are easily understood. There are people that talk in word clouds of language and take turns during a conversation that a Formula One driver could not follow. Reduce your word count and stay on track of the objective of the conversation. Do not stray and do not add any language or explanation that is not needed or requested. Communication richness is about the modality in which we communicate. In-person communication is the richest because it contains the words, non-verbal signals, and the tone of your voice or written material. Any other form of communication such as telephone or email reduces the richness significantly. In the history of our planet, no one has ever been complimented or acknowledged about her or his people skills because of email. When feasible, talk face-to-face and if not, schedule a virtual meeting or make a phone call. Face-to-face communication is the most impactful and meaningful because a great deal of the message shows up in non-verbal signals. Take your fingers off the keyboard and thumbs off the phone and make genuine human communication connections.

Beyond communication, the most noted and remembered people skill is about showing interest in others and making other people feel important. This will absolutely ensure that you are remembered and valued in return.

Asking About Someone is Respectful and Creates Lasting Connections

Shameless Plug Moment: In _LeadWell-The Ten Competencies of Outstanding Leadership_, there is a major section devoted to improving our ability to communicate and connect with others.

To grow and enhance your people skills, begin doing the following:

1. Valuing People
The beginning step in growing people skills is to intentionally value people beyond what they do for you or what they accomplish. Look deeper at the total person and what they add to their family, community, and the world. Take a long-term approach in establishing a person's value.

2. Mindfully and Intentionally Listen
Lock into every conversation as if someone were going to give you winning lottery numbers. Focus only on them and reduce any potential distraction and never try to multitask (a great myth) when engaged in listening. Never interrupt but ask clarifying questions and complimentary validate what you have heard (i.e., thank you for sharing that or that was very interesting).

3. Ask About Others
Demonstrate genuine interest in other people by asking what is important to them and what they value. Have you ever seen someone light up with a big smile and different tone when you ask about something important to them? That is because you asked. Let people have that feeling often and you will also be

surprised at how often they reciprocate and give you that great feeling of importance and value. If you're unsure about those items, start with family, pets, what they do in their free time, where they are from, and what they want to become or where they want to go. At each response, compliment their response to keep the information flowing and be sure to read item 4 below.

4.   Avoid Sharing or Oversharing Your Own Poetry
If you want to really demonstrate your prowess in people skills, you will learn to subordinate your own story and own things that you are just dying to share with others and make interactions about them. There will be plenty of time to tell your story but make interactions about other people as much as possible.

5.   Compliment and Appreciate People
When you see something in others that is a positive attribute or something you value, share it with them. Tell them you appreciate them or their efforts or their value. Tell them they did a great job or performed some work in an awesome manner. Do it in a genuine and enthusiastic way and do not keep those positive thoughts to yourself. If you see good, speak the good that you see.

6.   Non-Judgmental and Non-Comparing Empathy
Many interactions with people provide the opening for genuine empathy. Empathy is the placement of us in the scenario being experienced by another. This highly admired characteristic is about experiencing what they are feeling and understanding where they are. Two

important qualifiers separate good empathy from an awkward try. First, never compare the situation that someone is experiencing to something that has happened to you (i.e., you think that was bad, I was in the hospital for three days or sounds like a good camping trip like when we spent a month in Hawaii). Comparing makes it about you and not about them.

Eliminating judgement and fixing also set apart great empathy. Although your mind will be tempted to judge, and sometimes offer a fix for scenarios presented to you, you must not. It was not you and it is not about you, it is about them and they deserve empathy. Learn to say, "I am really sorry you are experiencing that" or "I really understand". Ask follow-up questions like how they feel about the situation and allow them to expand the conversation by showing additional interest.

7. Speak Ill of No One

Both your people skills and your reputation are on the line when you speak poorly or gossip about others. For most people, this is a significant turnoff that will alienate people and create no desire to speak with you again. If others try to draw you into their gossip or spreading of ill will, resist the temptation and say nothing or create some positive redirection for the conversation.

8. Use Courtesy

Sadly, please, thank you, and I'm sorry are becoming more and more rare in human interactions. Engage a platinum level of courtesy and error on the side of being overly polite. Appreciate (saying thank you) often, be courteous and gracious (say please always), and apologize to express empathy or regret. Be known as the politest person in the room. Please note there is an arcane stigma that courtesy equals weak. This could not be farther from the truth. Truly strong people are not afraid to be courteous and being viewed as nice. Only the insecure rely on arrogance and rudeness to try to demonstrate strength.

9. Let the Small Stuff Slide

Unless you live in an abandoned coal mine in West Virginia, you are going to encounter people during the day. During one or more of those interactions, someone is going to wrong you. They won't say hello back. They use the wrong words. They accidentally step on a sensitive issue for you. They do not pay enough attention to you. They do not text you back quick enough. You get the idea here; someone is going to slight you or not treat you exactly how you want to be treated.

Now the hard part; you must let those small little things go. Provide instant forgiveness and move on. Not dwell on it, do not retaliate, do not let it affect the other interactions you are going to have. Just let it go and move on, release it to the universe.

10. Do Not Seek Reciprocation

In a perfect world, every person you encounter would reciprocate all the above with you. Please do not be naïve and certainly do not engage in an interaction with someone and expect it back in return. It just will not happen. Your skills will invite the return to you and certainly model a great behavior but that is still no guarantee that it will come back to you. Treat any reciprocation of courtesy, interest in you, appreciation for you, or excellent listening as an unexpected bonus.

11. Smile

Nothing is most endearing and warm than a smile and it is one of the most powerful and easy to use people skills. Let them know you value the interaction with this simple non-verbal signal. Your smile will serve to attract people and people with a high level of energy to you. Not a cheesy grin, but a legitimate smile that shows you are happy to interact with them. Our facial expressions are common behavioral blind spots so you will need to be intentional about it until it becomes a more naturalized part of who you are.

12. A Little Energy

Even if you are a quiet, reserved, introvert, we need to add a little spark of energy to your interactions. No one wants to be engaged with someone who you can barely tell if they have a pulse or not. Speak up, smile, and add some great, positive energy to all your people interactions. Positive energy in people interactions will attract more of the same to you.

13. Prioritize People Interactions

We all get a little over-peopled at times. I do, my close friends do, we all do. We must be mindful that people are the most valuable resource around us. We are inherently connected to others. People are more important than projects, tasks, and really anything else we have going on. We need to prioritize those people interactions and opportunities for interactions ahead of the other stuff. It will still be there after you engage with people. I promise.

Lack of People Skills Frequency:
      Often   _____
      Occasionally   _____
      Never   _____

Lack of People Skills Impact:
      High   _____
      Moderate   _____
      Low   _____

Behavioral High Tendency: Dominance (D), Conscientiousness (C)
Behavioral Low Tendency: Influence (i), Steadiness (S)

Need to be Right and the Need to Win

"The need to be right is the sign of a vulgar mind."
Albert Camus

Again, Dr. Goldsmith pioneered the identification of this set of behaviors as being limiting and self-defeating.

We all like to be right. We like to win. We like to be acknowledged for being right and winning. Being right and winning, or at least the drive to win, has a place in our formula for success.

If you are the person that swats away the 8-yearold's shot at the basketball hoop, you may want to spend some time in this section. If you are the person that will argue about some miniscule point or inconsequential piece of data, you definitely want to spend time here.

The need to be right and win is an ego-based need, and our ego continues to feed this need. Consider the feeling you have when you are acknowledged for being right; it feels great. It feeds your ego and self-esteem and creates a cycle where you want to create that feeling again, again, and again. Winning creates the same cycle. Win once, absorb the feeling, enjoy the feeling, replicate the cycle.

Unfortunately, for you to be right and to win, someone else must be wrong and lose. This is an overlooked risk for those that are deeply entrenched in this defeating behavior. The need to be right and win creates casualty. An aside to remember is no one, and I mean no one, likes or likes to be around a know-it-all.

We all want to win but the successful people in the world create ways for everyone to win, creating a win-win scenario. A win without a loser.

Self-defeat comes when we place being right and winning above other values at the risk of losing relationships and alienating people. It also can connect to overthinking, especially when the issue is nonconsequential or meaningless. You can also see the need to be right appears in people's hyper-criticality and over-scrutiny of people and data.

Being Right Constantly Will Leave You Being Alone

Some people will use the need to be right to prove their value within an organizational structure or family environment.

Consider this scenario:

> Carla is challenged about a minor point of her department's performance. Rather than acknowledging the validity of the concern, she overwhelms the person questioning her with data and information justifying the performance issue. She clearly won the issue at hand but has alienated the

person posing the original concern and created a reputation for herself as being defensive and not open to any type of feedback. She was more interested in payback than being open.

The reputational damage done, and the relationships strained far outweigh the value of being right. Poor judgement.

Or another scenario:

> A fun family backyard game of badminton goes painfully bad when uncle Matt decides to spike the shuttlecock in the face of Grandma Denise. Matt and his partner won the point, but at what cost?

Matt obviously valued winning ahead of Grandma Denise.

And one more scenario to consider:

> Michelle, the accounts payable specialist, suspended the payment of an invoice because one date was listed incorrectly. She is absolutely correct about the error; however, the delay now causes delays in the delivery of a needed service from that vendor and strains that relationship.

Now here being right caused a strain in the relationship with a vendor and demonstrated a significant lack of judgement.

To turn down the need to win and be right, engage the following strategies:

1. Measure the Cost

When considering being right or winning the situation, consider the long-term costs associated with your action. Does being right outweigh the risk of damaged relationships? Does winning this situation have more value than letting it go? Quite bluntly, ask yourself if being right or winning is worth it.

2. Create Mutual Wins

Develop scenarios where others can be right or win as well. Don't make being right or winning as absolutes where there is one right and one wrong, one winner and one loser. This can be achieved simply by acknowledging the validity of a different perspective or appreciation of the different viewpoint. Let people know that you respect their view and have heard them.

3. Understand Proportionality and Scope

As previously discussed in length, not all details have the same value and weight. This is also true with the need to be right. If the issue is small and someone else can be right or win, let them. Forget your ego on the trivial and allow others the room to be right as well. They may not be but the feeling they will get from believing so is important to them. Learn to distribute your capital when a win and being right is important and let go of it when it is not.

4. Quit Associating Winning and Being Right

Being right and winning are not the same thing but sadly, many people associate them together. Often a win is achieved, especially a long-term win, when we acquiesce and accept being wrong, even if we are not.

There are many scenarios in interpersonal relationships when one person will admit to being wrong to achieve the long-term win of peace in the household or to make her or his partner feel better. Sometimes saying "you are right", even when they are not, will have much more value than remaining stuck in an argument over a meaningless detail. Make sure to manage your tone correctly so any "you are right" does not come across sarcastically or snidely.

One great example of this phenomenon is arguing with a baseball umpire about a bad ball and strike call. You may be right, but it won't end well for you. Take my word for it on this one.

Need to be Right and Win Frequency:
    Often   _____
    Occasionally   _____
    Never   _____

Need to be Right and Win Impact:
    High   _____
    Moderate   _____
    Low   _____

Behavioral High Tendency: Dominance (D), Conscientiousness (C), Influence (i) (occasionally)
Behavioral Low Tendency: Steadiness (S)

Bottlenecking

"In most organizations, the bottleneck is at the top of the bottle."
Peter Drucker

This is a particular defeating behavior that has its roots at work but also appears at home and can even paralyze an entire organization.

If you've ever heard of FOMO, or worse yet, been labeled with a FOMO tag, you will want to pay close attention to this section on bottlenecking. FOMO is an acronym for the fear of missing out. Not being in on the action. Not being connected to what everyone else is doing. Not being the approval source for all things.

The most perverse example that I have witnessed is (the names have been changed to protect the guilty):

> Ted is the assistant director at a major domestic airport. He is the public sector equivalent to a C-suite member of the private sector. He leads all airport operations not related to flights.
>
> Several hours a week, he manually reviews and approves all requests for time off for every team member in his division. All of them. Ted is the

assistant director and has associate directors, senior managers, managers, supervisors and team leads below him on the organizational chart, yet he finds it necessary to approve every request for a day off in his entire division of over 500 people.

The impact of this self-imposed bottleneck is easy to see. Team member requests for time off are delayed based on Ted's schedule. Direct supervisors are put in the awkward spot of not having the authority for a low-risk transaction involving their people. Ted is wasting valuable leadership time in this type of activity.

Ted wants to know the comings and goings. He wants to make sure his leaders are reviewing the requests. He has extreme FOMO and control freak issues. Ted has no idea how to effectively delegate, empower others, and let go of the reins. Ted also has not evolved in his leadership.

This type of behavior repeats itself thousands of times daily in organizations across the globe. Annual reviews require three approvals. Interviews have a panel of five people. Senior leaders must meet job candidates and on and on and on. All creating gross wastes of time and resources and slowing processes to a halt.

Another workplace example is:

When a teller is asked to waive a service fee because the deposit was not processed in a timely manner. The local financial institution, Bank of the US, requires a manager to review the request prior to waiving the fee.

For $10.00, the teller line is stalled, the manager's time is misallocated, and the teller wastes time finding the manager.

A little empowerment, understanding of true risk, and customer service principles would cure this situation.

Bottlenecking is not limited to the workplace. Consider this example from the home environment:

Matt and Veronica often work late at their respective jobs. Veronica offers to grab some chicken on the way home. Matt objects because he was not consulted on the choice or provided with other options.

Dinner is delayed and the message of trust in Veronica's choices is broken.

Do not get me wrong, collaboration, especially in interpersonal relationships, is very important and a characteristic of successful partnerships but there is such a thing as over-collaboration. When a vote is required for the most fundamental and easy household transactions, it is bottlenecked.

You Can Trust Others and Their Judgment

Bottlenecking can also create disempowerment among people, especially in the workplace. If they must ask permission or seek a second (and third, and fourth, and fifth) level of approval for everything, you are telling them that you do not trust them. If you hire smart people, empower them and let them go. Same at home. If you have smart people in your household and surround yourself with smart people, trust them and respect their decisions and judgements. All the bottlenecking that occurs sends messages of distrust and incompetence.

To reduce the impact of bottlenecking, engage these strategies:

1. Trust

Trust your team and family members to make good decisions and choices. Train and teach them about values and boundaries and let them operate with freedom within those constraints.

2. Create Limits and Tolerances

This is closely related to trust but more formalized. Create a list or grid of tolerances in which people can operate for routine transactions. Can they purchase $100.00 worth of supplies? Can they purchase a company car? Can they choose their own movie? Can they just leave for the weekend?

Document these tolerances, often based on the desire to take on risks and make sure they are appropriate to the level of team member or age of family member.

3. Empower Others

Give people a task, project, or some responsibility and then let them run with it. You do not need to know about every step they take. You do not need to be copied on the emails. You do not need to tell them how to do it. Trust them and let it go.

4.   Rely on Secondhand Reporting

You really do not need to see and hear everything firsthand, Doubting Thomas. Select a few reliable sources of information and stick with them. Trust their ability to deliver any news and information to you.

5.   Reduce Criticality and Skepticism

Some skepticism is healthy and keeps us from falling into traps. Likewise, critical thinking is a valuable skill. Both can be significantly overdone and cause bottlenecks. When we embrace acceptance, we allow people the room to grow and be successful without our constant questioning.

Bottlenecking Frequency:
     Often   _____
     Occasionally   _____
     Never   _____

Bottlenecking Impact:
     High   _____
     Moderate   _____
     Low   _____

Behavioral High Tendency: Dominance (D), Conscientiousness (C)
Behavioral Low Tendency: Influence (i), Steadiness (S)

Failure to Appreciate

"Happiness is found in the absence of expectation and the continuous focus on appreciation."
Tony Robbins

As a self-defeating behavior with far-reaching impact, the failure to appreciate can have large impacts on our relationships, how people view us, and our overall emotional health. As a comparison, a commitment to gratitude, both in attitude and in practice, can greatly enhance our lives and how we connect with others.

The most extreme form of the failure to appreciate shows up as a sense of entitlement. The belief that we are owed or due certain things and there is no need to express appreciation for them. It becomes a taking because we believe they should come to us and not being grateful for the presence of anything in our life.

For those of you in a leadership role at work, the failure to appreciate will result in a disengaged team and one that significantly underperforms. You will never become an admired leader without healthy doses of appreciation for your team members.

In interpersonal relationships, appreciation, even for the routine and mundane, keep love alive and ensure that resentments never creep in.

For a work-based example, consider:

> Edward leads a small team of twelve insurance agents for a major carrier. He never expresses any gratitude for the efforts or performance of his team. He has openly shared with them that their high-performance is what he expects and what he pays for in their salary.
>
> Shock best describes Edward's reaction when he receives the results of company-wide engagement survey. The scores paint a picture of a group in which no one wants to work for Edward, and many are actively looking for new jobs. The effort they provide is lower than what it could be because Edward does not appreciate any contribution from them. Edward is on the brink of losing his team.

Or an example from home:

> Kyle opens every door for Liz and walks her to her car every morning when she leaves for work. He provides Liz with an almost uncommon level of courtesy and respect and has done so for quite some time.
>
> Liz never says thank you for any of these gestures. In some cases, she pushes back on them but most commonly, she ignores them, almost expecting them to happen.

It does not take long for Kyle to begin to develop resentment about his efforts. He certainly wants to continue to do them, as he believes they show great value. With no reinforcement, he questions if this, and other efforts of his are wasted on the wrong person.

Appreciation is a powerful force that creates two significant benefits. When any effort, behavior, or performance is appreciated, it greatly increases the likelihood that it will be repeated. If you appreciate the work, they will repeat it. In some cases, they will even work harder to prove they can do even better and better.

There is No Greater Emotional Need than the Desire to be Appreciated and Valued

The second powerful force unlocked by appreciation is the self-esteem validation provided to someone else. We are ultimately not responsible for the self-esteem and ego of others, but we can certainly contribute to it in a powerful way by widely appreciating what others do for us. If you have ever seen someone's eyes light up when you appreciate them, you are witness to this effect in others. Their demeanor changes. Their faces begin to glow, and a smile replaces an apprehensive clenching of lips. They may even have a little extra energy in their step. You have made their day with a simple thank you.

You can improve your appreciation with these strategies:

1. Just Say Thank You
Get used to saying thank you. Whenever someone provides you with anything, even if it is their job or their role at home, appreciate what they provided. Get used to saying it a lot.

2. Look for the Good
Purposefully and intentionally, look for the good in others and in what they do. Stop being so anxious to be critical or provide suggestions for improvement (see the prior section on hyper-criticality) and look for what is right and what you value. If you can see it, you can say it. Learn to find what is working well and build upon that.

3. Commit to Expression
Most people, or many at least, do a pretty good job of seeing the good around them. There are certainly exceptions, but many do note and make a mental entry of when they see something good, or even great. What is lacking however is committing to expressing these observations to a verbal expression of gratitude and appreciation. When you see good, commit to verbalizing it or sending an appreciation note as a priority, and not when time allows. If you think back to our elementary school years, they promoted catching people doing good and then appreciating that.

4. Practice Gratitude
The skills for appreciation are natural for some but need to be developed for many others. For those of you, like me, in which it is not naturalized, we need to work on the practice of gratitude.

This is more than the discipline of just saying thank you or sending an appreciation note; this is a mindset change brought on through intentional practice. To begin, create a notebook or journal for gratitude. List five things daily in which you are thankful, or you appreciated. Asterisk or denote one item of the five that you commit to sharing with the person that performed the act in which you are grateful. Be sure to list at least one of the five items in which you appreciated your own actions. Yes, be grateful for something that you have done.

This practice needs to be repeated for at least 40 days, every day, without fail for any mindset or attitude shift to occur.

Failure to Appreciate Frequency:
    Often   _____
    Occasionally   _____
    Never   _____

Failure to Appreciate Impact:
    High   _____
    Moderate   _____
    Low   _____

Behavioral High Tendency: Dominance (D), Conscientiousness (C)
Behavioral Low Tendency: Influence (i), Steadiness (S)

Not Seeking or Accepting Feedback

"Feedback is the breakfast of champions."
John Maxwell

Many people will profess an openness to feedback, or even halfheartedly ask for it, but few really embrace the value of feedback and create mechanisms to solicit it.

Failure to obtain meaningful feedback from others creates this vacuum in which our total self-view is based on our own thoughts and opinions. In turn, which produces a false narrative about us that ranges from falsely negative or overly inflated. In short, we either see ourselves as worse than we really are or much better than we really are and nothing close to the reality of who we are. To frame this another way, we often build self-beliefs and self-esteem around who we want to be and not who we really are.

Consider who really knows you the best. When we are self-honest and open, we realize it is not ourselves. It is the people around us. It is our significant other. It is our co-worker. It is our best friend. It is the team we lead. Sometimes it is your boss or other stakeholders in your life. Creating systems to solicit and capture feedback from others will help you create a much more accurate view of yourself and allow you to work on the right things moving forward.

You Are Not Who You Think You Are

A couple of examples about the need for feedback or the impact of the lack of feedback:

> Ed is not a well-liked supervisor. He has a harsh tone of voice and tends to raise it when mildly aggravated or upset. Ed is entirely unaware of this, and he believes he is simply projecting a passionate approach to situations. Unfortunately, his team hears it as being rude, harsh and demanding. Ed has never asked for feedback about his tone.

> A handful of his team has complained to Ed's boss about him, and a few have filed grievances with their union or the human resources department. Ed is in trouble and does not have a clue about the reasons.

As bad as not seeking feedback from others, rebutting it, disagreeing with it, or disputing it is worse. Consider this example:

> Kim has crafted a self-belief of near infallibly. She knows all, sees all, and has a solution to every problem, even when not invited to share it.

> She has received feedback on several occasions but always knows better and always disputes the validity of the observations. This has created a relationship dynamic with others in which no one will provide her with any valuable feedback. Kim continues to dismiss the information provided to her and live in the perfect fantasy world of her own creation.

In turn, this has also contributed to her becoming rigid, inflexible, and completely closed to any difference of view or opinion. It is her way or no way.

And a final example from the home front:

> Lisa has received feedback, in a thoughtful manner, about her shutting down and not communicating whenever there is a disagreement or argument in the household. Not only does she not act on the feedback, but she also justifies the behavior by saying that is how she copes and really does not want to hear it anymore. Robert, her husband, has always tried to deliver feedback to Lisa in a thoughtful and respectful manner, but he has had enough pushback and has built up some significant resentment in ever giving Lisa any feedback again. Certainly not a healthy relationship dynamic. Robert is shutting down and withdrawing from communication with Lisa.

To improve the acceptance and solicitation of feedback, begin to:

1. Feedback Partner
Get yourself someone in your life that will be honest with you and provide you with the feedback you need. Somone that will root for you, tell you when you have done well, encourage you when you need it, and most importantly, tell you where you have challenges and flaws. Someone who just tells you the good is not useful although we tend to migrate to those people.

We need someone who will be truly honest in both the good and the bad.

This person can be found in any segment of your life. You must be scrutinizing in reference to the motives of who you want to provide feedback. Are they legitimately interested in you becoming a better person? Do they have your best interests at heart? Or perhaps are there ulterior motives to providing you feedback like overly inflating you or tearing you down for their own gratification?

Often those closest to us are not the best feedback partners. Because they want to sustain and maintain the relationship with you, they will hold back on some of the critical or challenging feedback we need desperately. Siblings, best friends, or trusted peers usually make great feedback partners.

2. Deflate Your Narrative

We all craft a narrative of ourselves that is not based on a ton of reality. The most commonly self-created narrative is built on what we would like to be and not who we really are. We must develop the self-honesty to know that my self-beliefs are not accurate, and we need feedback to reconcile to the reality of who I am.

3. Solicit Feedback

Ask the people in your life, your key stakeholders, how you are doing. Openly ask for the good, okay, and the areas that need work. Do not overthink this process. Simply ask people "how am I doing", "what can I do better", "what can I work on", "what should I do more of", or "what should I do less of". Ask very open-ended questions to get the most data from the response.

Care should be taken not to shop for feedback that you like or shop for a feedback source that gives you nothing but agreement and what you want to hear. Some will shop their desire for specific feedback until they find the person or people who totally support them and see nothing wrong with their behaviors. You want honesty, not a poll showing how righteous you are.

4. Graciousness of Acceptance
When you receive feedback, by all means, be gracious in the acceptance of it. Never pushback, justify, or excuse the feedback you are receiving. Even if you do not like it or even if you do not find it particularly accurate, just appreciate it. It is likely that some of what you might find as not accurate is a behavioral blind spot (known to others, but not you) or a perception in which you are creating the behavioral projection. Watch for veiled pushback that often shows up in a request for an example. Even that request for clarification can dry up the feedback source in the future. People who choose to provide us feedback should be valued and appreciated, not forced into lengthy narratives about what they are seeing or sensing. At the very least, accept what they are saying as perception, even if you cannot see the reality of it.

Just say thank you, process the information later.

5. Acceptance of Self
We are not as good as we think we are, and we are not as bad as we think we are. Self-honesty requires us to look at ourselves with the lens of a balanced scorecard. We all have some very good characteristics and behaviors, and we all have things we could do better or improve upon. This is all part of being human, the good and the opportunities for improvement. No one is perfect and no one is totally flawed. We are a beautiful mix.

Failure to Accept or Solicit Feedback Frequency:
    Often   _____
    Occasionally   _____
    Never   _____

Failure to Accept or Solicit Feedback Impact:
    High   _____
    Moderate   _____
    Low   _____

Behavioral High Tendency: Dominance (D), Conscientiousness (C),
Behavioral Low Tendency: Influence (i), Steadiness (S)

Being Extra

"Being extra nice to someone can be a form of manipulation; kindness is an exercise of power in its own right."
Wang Anyi

Extra ice cream. Free refills. Extra innings. Upgrades to business class. Yes, please. Every time, every day.

The same with extra kindness, extra nice, extra politeness, and extra patience. All valuable extras.

Extra, unnecessary words and explanations, unsolicited advice, suggestions that do not really add any true value, hyper-emotionalism in interactions, and passive-aggressive bragging are all forms of limiting and defeating extras.

But sometimes people become extra and there is no value to their extra-ness, and it serves to rebuff people and push them away. The interesting part of this phenomenon is that people being overly extra rarely know they are doing it and never know the impact of their actions. One of the more important damages to consider is that extra people do not invite future interactions but rather people will tend to avoid them. In any circumstance this can be very limiting and defeating.

I absolutely love the Urban Dictionary's definition of being extra. They define it as being over the top, excessive, dramatic behavior, and my favorite piece, doing the absolute damn most for no reason. Being extra is going to cover a broad swath of behaviors and habits, many of which are unknown to the doer, but painfully clear to those around them.

Here again, the credit for breaking the ground goes to Marshall Goldsmith and the self-defeating behavior he identified is Adding Value. Dr. Goldsmith uses multiple examples of leaders providing suggestions to team member's ideas thusly depreciating the value of the idea and sucking the morale out of that team member. This piece of being extra also reduces the likelihood that the team member will ever share another idea. Devastating self-defeat and rarely known to the person doing it.

Let Other People Keep the Spotlight and Credit

Some people mask this behavior under the heading of "trying to be helpful" and they truly believe that, but what they don't see is the impact of those actions on others. Consider a couple of examples:

> Terri proudly shares the results of her detailed analysis with her boss, Thomas. Thomas acknowledges the good work then, without taking as much as a pausing breath, proceeds to share with Terri some suggestions on font size, column spacing, and tab colors. None of those items impact the overall value of the analysis and

associated reports and most are simply Thomas' preferences or the way he would have done it.

Terri's initial reaction of pride in her work is immediately deflated but she says nothing. Thomas thinks he is being helpful.

Or another example:

Kelley delivers a great four-hour training class. She asks her boss, Tim, how she did, and Tim expresses some praise then follows it immediately with what he would have done or said. Again, with the camouflage of helpfulness, Tim deflates Kelley, and she completely feels defeated.

(Hmmmm. I wonder where this example is from?)

And one final example of extra to consider:

You are seeing Brenda for the first time in a very long time. She gushes to the point of tears about how great it is and how much she loves, loves, loves, and loves even more the interaction and time together. She then follows that up with a series of Facebook Messenger notes reiterating the same. Over-the-top? Absolutely and uncomfortably so.

You can probably provide dozens of examples of these things happening to you and maybe even some in which you did it to another person. This phenomenon is not limited to the working world, we also do it to our kids, also under the guise of being helpful.

There are some other types of being extra to consider as well. Being extra can come in the form of someone who uses way too many words in all interactions. Some people are naturally wordier and more verbose than others but the truly extra take this to an artform. They will absolutely drone a conversation and make it, unintentionally, very one-sided. A simple word count will yield at least a 2 to 1 ratio of words and in some cases, 3 to 1, 4 to 1, or 5 to 1. This happens in person and in email and text exchanges.

Extra people also show themselves in over-the-top emotionalism. They will lavish and heap praise and other mush when simpler, and more concise phrases will have more impact. The extra folk also seem addicted to emoticons to add even more extra. I had the displeasure of having a fringe in law a few years ago that could not write a single sentence and one without the dripping of emotion that would make most soap opera characters uncomfortable. Five thank yous, six loves, four omgs, and three smiley faces would compose her typical Facebook message. Absolutely unreadable and credibility destroyed. Yes, she was wordier than most, but this was extra beyond wordy. There was not a social media post that did not have a response from her within 3 seconds of posting. Extra squared.

Over-the-top extraness is not limited to the hyperbole of positive situations. People can also be extra when faced with obstacles, challenges, and setbacks. This Chicken Little phenomenon of the sky falling at every minor road bump is a very difficult one to be around. They will tend to highly exaggerate the impact of failure and the impact of things like budget cuts, a new boss showing up, or any other relatively common change.

Being extra also shows up in people that love to show off how smart they are and everything they know. For trivia night at the neighborhood tavern, this is awesome, and this person needs to be on your team. For all other settings, this can create significant disconnects and harm the desire of people to interact with you moving forward. You will hear phrases like "in my previous job", "based on my experience", or "my research tells me" that are about to lead into someone about to share way too much extra about how smart they are. No one likes a know-it-all. This type of extra will also show itself with million-dollar vocabulary words, again designed to show intelligence without regard to potential disconnects with others. We know you are smart; you do not need to remind us constantly.

Another type of extra is found in people who just cannot help but provide leading explanations. So instead of asking "would you please move your truck", they launch into a lengthy diatribe about all the reasons for moving the truck, the lack of prior knowledge of the need to move the truck, and the consequences of not moving the truck. All of that is highly unnecessary and convolutes the needed action of moving the truck. These types of people need to trust that if someone has questions about their directive or inquiry, they will ask. Frontloaded explanations will confuse people greatly and even lose a big chunk of listeners.

If you have ever heard someone leading into a conversation with "if you do not mind me saying", you're about to be extra'd in another way. Unsolicited feedback and advice are common forms of being extra. This type of extra can become especially annoying and lead to some damaged relationships and overall avoidance. Please remember, unless you are invited to provide feedback, just don't.

A final indicator of being extra is the need to always have the final word. They say goodbye, you say goodbye, and then they must add a see you soon. Even in email, you say thank you and you get a note back moments later that says "no, thank you." Just being extra for extras sake.

To cure being extra, begin:

1. Be More Direct
Consciously and mindfully use less language especially the language that is unimportant and does not add legitimate value. Pay close attention to the amount of qualifier words you use such as feel, believe, seems, and think. These words distract from any importance and credibility of your message and are unnecessary fillers. Also watch for hyperbole in your communication and avoid expressions like "absolute very best", "most excellent", "super-fantastic" and the like. These have no value and again, reduce overall communication credibility.

A more direct communication approach will also be achieved by maintaining the focus on the purpose of your communication. Stick solely to what you are trying to convey and avoid taking the wild left and right-hand turns that become impossible to follow and comprehend. Save your storytelling for the campfire,

Uncle Bob's birthday party, and mentoring your successor.

2.   Just Say Thank You

Stop adding your two cents worth when not invited or when that two cents will cause much more devaluation. Validate the work and ideas of others with the simple appreciation of a sincerely delivered "thank you". Stay away from any suggestions, any redirections of what else they could add or think about, and any reference to how you would have done it. Just thank you. Nothing more and nothing less.

3.   Ask Permission

Before you tell the neighbor that she is mowing the grass wrong or tell the certified mechanic how to work on your car, ask permission to provide feedback or guidance. Now if they greenlight your input, share away, but if you detect hesitancy or they say any form of no, keep your commentary to yourself, no matter how helpful it may seem.

Even when coaching team members in a working environment and especially with peer level people, always engage this as a best practice. This also will aid the flow of communication in coaching events and give you guidance on the receptiveness of other people to your suggestions.

Likewise, if you have some ideas or comments on someone else's ideas or innovation, use this same approach. Never just jump in with a "you should try" statement. Ask first to participate in their creativity.

4. Seek Feedback

As indicated previously, most extra people do not have a clue that they are being extra or the impact of their "extraness". To see if you are one of the extra providers, ask people around you. There will be more about seeking feedback in Section III of this book, but simply learn to ask if you are being extra and validate any feedback with the simple thank you described above. You may not always love the feedback, but it is solid gold to your growth and improvement.

5. Limit Emotional Expressions

Emotional expression is necessary and important, but this can be overdone quickly. Limit how much emotionalism you include in all modalities of communication. Does one heart emoticon express love? Do you need to add four of them? Probably not.

6. Take Your Hands Off the Keyboard

You do not need to validate every response that comes to your inbox or in your message folder. Say thank you when needed but stop redundant replies or echoing other people's replies of a similar, or same nature.

Being Extra Frequency:
    Often   _____

    Occasionally   _____

    Never   _____

Being Extra Impact:
    High   _____

    Moderate   _____

    Low   _____

Behavioral High Tendency: Influence (i), Conscientiousness (C)
Behavioral Low Tendency: Dominance (D), Steadiness (S)

Avoiding the Unpleasant

"Everything you want is on the other side of fear."
Jack Canfield

There are things in life that are just plain and simply unpleasant. Gross to think about even. Nothing fun or attractive about them or doing what you have to with them. Cleaning the kid's bathroom. Taking care of the kitty litterbox (my oldest son wore a bandana around his face when it was his turn to do this at my house), talk to the office curmudgeon about how he treats people, talk to the spouse about money, call the upset customer back. None of those are fun but all of them are necessary.

Avoidance of the unpleasant, or the more commonly perceived unpleasant, is caused by fear. In turn that fear is either driven by the history of actual experiences with that unpleasant person or situation or the self-created belief that the person or situation will be bad. Either way it creates fear of tackling the undesirable situation. In some people, this fear can be totally paralyzing.

We all, or certainly most of us, have things we tend to avoid because they are unpleasant, or at least, we believe them to be unpleasant. Unfortunately, as discussed with procrastination, there can be significant lost opportunity when we avoid confronting the unpleasant. Those opportunities can range from the improved performance of a team member to a clearing of the air with your significant other. Avoidance does not make anything better and simply risks any of the positive outcomes from addressing the situation.

Tackling the Unpleasant Creates Room for More Enjoyment

You will also notice, either in yourself or others, that the overuse of humor (my hand is raised), laughter, or sarcasm creates coverage for dealing with the unpleasant. The use of humor in inappropriate situations (think funerals or serious meetings) is a tagalong symptom of this behavioral trait. This behavior is a classic avoidance technique or at least used to take an edge off things we do not want to deal with. When the situation calls for seriousness, we need to be able to self-manage ourselves and summon it.

Consider this all-too-common workplace example:

> From a core performance and technical expertise perspective, Julio does his job just fine and meets all documented performance standards. Unfortunately, he is a horrible human to deal with and Carrie, his manager, is constantly getting complaints about him from the rest of the team and other key stakeholders. These complaints all have the common theme of him being rude, obnoxious, talking down to people, and becoming argumentative when anyone disagrees with him.

Carrie knows that she has to address this or risk her credibility with the rest of the team or maybe even have some of them leave because of Julio. In prior attempts to discuss his behavior, Julio has become defensive and pushed back in a very forceful way.

Rather than taking the courageous approach of discussing Julio's behavior in a direct manner with a clear iteration of interpersonal expectations, Carrie chooses to ignore the situation because of its perceived discomfort and even goes as far as to make excuses for Julio to other team members.

The scenario above, the failure to provide corrective feedback when required costs a lot more than Julio's performance. At stake here and at real risk is the rest of the team. They will become disengaged and perhaps even leave the organization because of this leadership failure.

And now an example from the home front:

Sarah struggles with her boyfriend Matt's use of social media. He posts way too much information and overshares personal details that should best be left between them. She is very uncomfortable about this and wants to strike a more private mode for their relationship.

As much as she is uncomfortable with Matt's use of social media, she is more uncomfortable with confronting him directly about. She has dropped hints from time-to-time, and Matt has failed to pick up on them. Now Sarah has become resentful, and the issue is much bigger in their relationship.

A little courage in this example would have saved the build-up of resentment and could easily have been solved early with a more direct, and fear-free approach. Other home-based examples could be about talking about money, bad habits, or even a couple's sex life. In all those cases the fear of a reaction or the perceived fear of a reaction or fear of a confrontation keeps those discussions from occurring when they should. Many people also are afraid of the judgement of other people, both those close to them, and total strangers.

Successful, happy people, and certainly successful leaders, confront the uncomfortable daily, all the time. You cannot achieve success unless you are willing to look difficult situations directly in the eye and deal with them in a timely manner. Happiness and success are not found in avoiding the unpleasant but rather in dealing with the unpleasant quickly and with a good attitude. Quite simply, success, in any endeavor, requires comfort with the uncomfortable.

To improve dealing with uncomfortable situations and people, engage the following:

1. Assess the Risk
As mentioned earlier in reference to procrastination, we must take an honest view of the actual risks involved and be willing to challenge our self-imposed risk factors that are not supported by direct history. Eliminate the self-talk that creates doubt and unreasonable views of risk.

2. Prioritize the Unpleasant

One of the easiest strategies for dealing with difficult or unpleasant situations is to do them first. Get them out of the way and make the rest of the day better by comparison. Have the coaching session first thing. Return that difficult customer call immediately. This also helps you avoid overthinking and making up crazy reasons not to do the unpleasant.

3. Reframe Your Expectation

Many people self-create expectations of a negative outcome. Not only do those work to craft the actual outcome but they also are largely never true. Openly and intentionally set an expectation of a positive outcome. Tell yourself that it will go well, or it will be fun instead of the opposite.

4. Reward Yourself

When you tackle an unpleasant task or situation, give yourself a little reward. Maybe a little time off, a few silly cat videos, frilly coffee drink, or even just a short break. Looking forward to a reward or treat can often get you over the hump to tackle the unpleasant.

Avoiding the Unpleasant Frequency:
    Often   _____
    Occasionally   _____
    Never   _____

Avoiding the Unpleasant Impact:
    High   _____
    Moderate   _____
    Low   _____

Behavioral High Tendency: Steadiness (S), Influence (i), Conscientiousness (C)
Behavioral Low Tendency: Dominance (D)

Wasting Time

"A man who dares to waste one hour of time has not discovered the value of life."
Charles Darwin

When we are young, we look at time as nearly infinite. There will always be time to get something done, to achieve something meaningful, to take that dream trip. As we get older, that sense of time becomes more compressed, and we realize that time is fleeting. The saddest comments I have ever heard are regrets. The "I wish I would have", or "I wish I could have" are incredibly sad to hear especially when you consider a better use of time could have achieved what is now a regret. My sincere wish is you never have an "I wish I would have" statement come from your mouth.

We all need a little downtime. We all need a little break. We all need some time when we can turn off our brain and just chill. Rest is an important part of being successful and healthy. That being said, we do need to be on guard and aware of when our use of time becomes wasteful and self-defeating. We also need to look closely at some of our habits and routines to ensure that they are serving us well, not just chewing up valuable time.

Rest and Self-Care are Valuable Uses of Time

Time wasting comes in all shapes and sizes. It can be watching kitten videos on TikTok for hours on end, it can be personal habits like smoking, it can be endlessly chasing a rabbit down a hole for a meaningless piece of information, it can be spending hours working on an insignificant issue or problem (perfectionists), it can be our own vanities, and it can be the amount of time spent pondering (overthinkers). Our challenge becomes what becomes a needed therapeutic piece of distraction or down time or what becomes truly a waste of our most precious resource.

Consider these few workplace examples:

> Tim (strange coincidence) needs a little mental break and decides to check out a few funny and cute videos on TikTok. He tells himself that he is only going to do that for ten minutes to recharge his brain a bit. A full hour later, he is still scrolling videos and even searching some hashtags that made him laugh.

This is an easy example of wasted time, especially when repeated regularly. A little self-discipline here would have cured this time parasite.

Another relatively common example from work:

> Priscilla, the company's Chief Financial Officer spends three hours looking for a $7.15 discrepancy in a little used general ledger account. After reviewing records from 2015 to current, she decides that she is going to have to dig deeper to resolve this.

Not only is this a waste of time, but it is also a breach of responsibility in using her company's resources correctly. The amount of her time spent on an insignificant amount is grotesque.

One final work example is:

> Rod accepts all meeting requests and never applies any critical thought to the meeting subject, why he has been invited, and if there is anyone else who could or is attending that could disseminate the information. At the end of almost every day, Rod is frustrated that his entire day has been eaten by meetings and he has achieved little. Rod's meetings have become a significant waste of his time.

We need to spend a little time talking about addictions. Not the dark ones like alcoholism or substance abuse but addictions related to how we use time.

There is a healthy group of people that are addicted to being busy. In fact, they often appear overwhelmed with what they have going on. They are constantly rushed, which harms the relationship with others, never have time for anything meaningful, and never really have anything to show for all their busyness. They either feign or experience genuine burnout because of their addiction to being busy. Business addiction is pervasive.

Another interesting addiction to examine relates to self-care. Some people have taken the need for self-care to an addictive level. Yoga in the morning. Gym at lunchtime. Running in the early afternoon. Stretching and boxing class in the evening.

From a day, they are devoting half or more to self-care routines. While self-care is extremely important and necessary, it cannot dominate your life. When overdone, self-care of any type will become aloof and unapproachable, and the self-care addict will have no time for the needs of others.

To better manage your time and reduce the amount of wasted time, try the following:

1. Time and Task Matching

One of the great skills of time management is to balance the time available with the tasks that need completion. It makes no sense to have a to do list of 15 items and you are tied up in meetings all day. Time and task matching forces us to think about placing the tasks into time slots, days, weeks, and months in which the time allows. This also helps relieve a great deal of stress related to undone tasks and projects.

2. Prioritize

So much time is frittered away on working on the unimportant. This is a great tactic of those that are addicted to busyness. Layout your projects and tasks in an order that matches what is truly a priority. Sometimes this will be done by the due date but more effective is to devote time to what is a necessity.

3. Identify and Attack the Parasites

Time parasites, those nasty creatures that suck away valuable time, come in all shapes and sizes. Web surfing, overly connected to the mobile phone, games, interruptions, funny videos, vanity tasks (those things we like to do but really have no value), and our personal habits are just some examples. Take some time, identify the parasites, estimate the time they suck away from you each day or week, then apply some strategies and common sense to minimize the impact. You may never fully eliminate your time parasites, but you can certainly reduce their drag on your time.

4. Plan and Create Deadlines

The use of deadlines and the associated planning will keep you from spinning your wheels or the hamster running on a wheel phenomenon. When you break larger projects into smaller pieces with deadlines, the project gets completed easily and without any feelings of being overwhelmed by the scope of the project. Deadlines also force you to be disciplined in your approaches to the required tasks.

5. Look at Your Habits and Routines

Some of our habits and routines serve us extremely well. Some certainly do not. Look at all the things you do repetitively and see which ones still serve you and see which ones need modification or elimination. Often new habits are needed in order to grow and move ahead and to make room for the new, we must abandon the old habits and routines.

Wasting Time Frequency:
    Often   _____
    Occasionally   _____
    Never   _____

Wasting Time Impact:
    High   _____
    Moderate   _____
    Low   _____

Behavioral High Tendency: Steadiness (S), Influence (i)
Behavioral Low Tendency: Dominance (D), Conscientiousness (C)

Section III – Growth Attitudes and Mindsets Replaces Our Negative Attitudes and Beliefs

Behaviors are those actions that are seen and observable by the outside world. They are known by others, known by you, and sometimes, in the case of blind spots, not known by you. Conversely, attitudes and beliefs are not seen by the outside world until they begin being projected in your behavior or in sets of behaviors. All our behaviors are driven by our attitudes and beliefs.

The coolest and best thing about attitudes and beliefs is that we have a choice on which ones we will embrace and drive our behaviors. Every day, we get to choose our belief set and make the conscious and intentional choice to not let any person or outside events influence our choice of attitude. This is our superpower. We get to choose our attitudes and beliefs. Choose wisely.

There are certainly a set of those attitudes and beliefs that are self-limiting and self-defeating. This is especially true when these beliefs and attitudes leak out in our behavior. Unlike the behaviors in previous sections, there is no reliable correlation between any personality types or behavioral styles and the prevalence of these beliefs and attitudes. There is also no way to correctly measure or assess the severity of impact of these attitudes either. We will only be looking at how often these occur within you.

None of us is made up of a single attitude or belief and we often combine elements of several that drive our behaviors. Although, there will always be one dominant attitude that produces most of our actions and behaviors. We want to create a positive primary or driving attitude and belief set as well as several healthy supporting beliefs and attitudes.

The work on our behaviors is relatively straightforward. Not always easy but simple and qualitative. Working on attitudes is a bit more complex and requires us to make a shift into a new attitude set purposefully and intentionally.

The limiting attitudes and beliefs we will work on in this section include:
Flexibility and Openness
Forgiving and Healed
Abundance
Positive Expectations
Optimistic and Upbeat
People and Experience Legacy
Confidence and Humility
Resilience
Productive and Peaceful
Excellence (Not Perfection)
Genuine and Transparent
Ownership and Accountability

The Attitude Buffet

"No one else can choose your attitude for you. Your perspective and choice of attitude gives you the power to be in control."
Irene Dunlap

As a long-term resident of the Las Vegas area, I know a thing or two about buffets. Two deserts; yes, please. Prime rib and smoked brisket; yes, indeed. Pass on the green vegetables; absolutely. The buffet is the ultimate exercise in getting things your way. More of what you like, double of what you love, and less of what doesn't work for you.

Attitudes and beliefs have the same dynamics. You get to choose pieces from all the good attitude and beliefs sets and make a very uniquely your attitude package. As you read the below set of beliefs and attitudes, you can add them as you want and create your own customized attitude.

As a best practice, I recommend that you intentionally select two or three driving attitudes for each day. Make it an intention that you will select openness, positive, and forgiving. You can create any combination that you want and soon enough it will become automatic for you to select your customized attitude package. Any two or three good ones will work, and the important point is that you are intentional about it, and you lock it in your mind for that day. As the day progresses, remind yourself of the three-attitude package you have created and reset your attitudes as needed.

Some people have found it helpful to note and journal the three-attitude intention for the day. This practice helps reinforce what you want to be feeling and believing during the day.

The buffet is a good thing. The crafting, and daily embracing, of a customized attitude and belief set is an awesome thing.

Flexibility and Openness Replaces Hyper-Rigidity

"A rigid mind is very sure but often wrong. A flexible mind is generally unsure, but often right."
Vanda Scaravelli

With openness and flexibility, a great abundance of possibility comes to us. When we are open and flexible to different outcomes, we get to see great parts of the world around us and create deeper connections with people. We can truly feel more and create less resistance to the path in front of us.

Openness and flexibility will make us significantly more open to change, even when we have no input into those change events. An attitude and belief centered on flexibility and openness will also reduce our natural tendencies to be harshly judgmental of others. By being open, we will accept different view, different appearances, different values and different approaches. This reduction in negative and harsh judgments will in turn have a positive impact on your physical and emotional health. You feel better and have better emotional energy when you stop carrying the negative judgements we often place on others and on situations. Go with the flow, adopt acceptance of all, and feel better because of it.

Open and flexible will also eliminate any hate for other people or situations. When we are truly open, hatred becomes impossible, no matter how bad we perceive the actions or events. We may still dislike it, but we will certainly not abhor it.

We all know them. Some of them are our relatives, close friends, co-workers, or even our boss. The soul that is so rigid in their thinking that they leave no room for any other possibilities or any other outcomes. They have developed an absolutism about a wide range of subjects ranging from how to work, how relationships are supposed to play out, to darker views about people and the world.

Rigidity shows itself in absolutism of beliefs and related communication and action. There is no flexibility or thought about another perspective or view. During political and football seasons this shows up in spades. Try talking to a Packer fan about the Dallas Cowboys or try to have a reasonable discussion with a fully committed member of the other political party. Absolutism and rigidity are on full display. Good luck to you with those engagements.

Rigid beliefs and attitudes become self-defeating when they refuse to allow other possibilities or options. When a person's attitudes and beliefs exclude the potential of another view, it significantly narrows any possibility of outcomes. In its most extreme form, hyper-rigidity will create strains in both work and personal relationships and people will often avoid those people who have demonstrated rigidity in their actions and words. People will avoid you and work around you instead of with you.

Hyper-rigidity is often driven by biases, both known and unknown. The most frequent bias driver for hyper-rigidity is confirmation bias. This is where a person only searches for and accepts evidence that supports their position and openly shuns any other view or perspective. Confirmation bias, in and of itself, is extremely limiting to any person both professionally and personally and can lead to very poor decisions and judgements.

Rigid, unbending beliefs and attitudes also show up in how we view people. Far too often we either look at people as being all good or all bad and nothing in between, which is the accurate view. We will view another family member, co-worker, or friend as being perfect and dismiss any evidence of the contrary. This is named confirmation bias and is very common in people. Similarly, we will view someone as being fatally flawed based on some limited evidence, then judge them harsher than they should be, ignoring all evidence to the contrary. No one is all good. No one is all bad. There is bad with the good and good with the bad.

Openness Unlocks Possibilities

We all need some rigidity in our values, morals, and ethics. Everyone has some solid beliefs and attitudes that they carry throughout major parts of their life. Everything else should be subject to flexibility, critical thinking, and self-examination.

The substitute belief and mindset is flexibility and openness. To be open, truly open, you must learn to consider all perspectives before dismissing any for your own view and approach. A flexible and open mindset is open to almost all possibilities and outcomes and becomes a powerful life driver, especially when combined with optimism. The attitude of flexibility and openness will expose you to greater potential, better solutions, and enhanced relationships with others.

To begin shifting to a flexible and open attitude, begin:

1. Apply Critical Thinking
Critical thinking is a much more disciplined way of thinking that requires analysis, evaluation, interpretation, and review of information sources. It also often requires skeptical questioning of the sources and validity of data. When we engage critical thinking, we can often dispel common dogmas and certainly reduce the amount of any absolutism. Good critical thinkers also challenge their own assumptions and beliefs regularly. They look at decisions and look for alternatives and different approaches.

2. Look for Options and Different Perspectives
For every option presented or for the direction that you think is best, look for alternatives and different paths that create the same or similar outcomes. There is not just one road to Rome and there are many ways to come to a desired result. Just because it was your first thought, or the one you may be most comfortable with, does not mean it's the only way to achieve what is needed. We also tend to fall in love with a path when it's our idea and become automatically dismissive when another approach is offered. That, in and of itself, is extremely limiting and defeating.

3. Apply Empathy

The ever-rarer application of human empathy requires us to put ourselves in the situation, or the emotional condition, of another person and see from their eyes, hear from their ears, and feel from their feelings. When we pause and apply some empathy, we can more clearly see different perspectives and compromise to another position, or at least admit its possible or plausible.

4. Compromise

Many people with absolute and rigid beliefs do not know how to compromise. Compromise openly and freely to allow everyone to win and get a voice into a process. This does not mean you have to give away important positions, but you can certainly give ground when the details are meaningless to the bigger outcome. Learn to create mutual wins instead of the hollow wins associated with your rigid position.

5. Listen

Those with absolute and rigid attitudes often do not listen to other perspectives and actively tune them out. They may hear but not listen to anything that does not match their narrative of how something should be (confirmation bias). Remove your preconceived ideas about a subject, put your rebuttal in park, and listen (or read) another side of the story.

6.   Confront Your Confirmation Bias

Openly challenge your desire to use and migrate to only confirming information. Look for balance in the information and don't dismiss anything that does not nicely fit with the narrative you have created about a situation or a person. Create a balanced view. Confirmation bias is a very limiting thought pattern and needs to be intentionally confronted when it appears.

7.   Practice

Practice flexibility and openness with small things. As it becomes easier with things like where to have dinner or what car to take, the bigger ones will become easier too.

Forgiving and Healed Replaces Unforgiven and Unhealed Wounds

"When a deep injury is done to us, we never recover until we forgive."
Alan Paton

Healed and free from past wrongs and slights is a great place to be. It is absolutely amazing to not haul around heavy loads when we feel wronged or hurt. It is the state and condition we were born into. There is a purity of our minds and emotions when we are healed and have forgiven the wrongs of others. Healed and free from the baggage of past wrongs, no matter how bit or small, is our target belief and attitude.

Letting go of things, those wrongs and hurts, sound overly simple and it is. Ultimately, that is what we need to do. Healing the wounds and forgiving the past wrongs is our target to create the space for new experiences and growth. Healing and forgiveness also help us avoid the bitterness and jadedness often associated with unhealed or unforgiven wounds and wrongs. It will also help us be more transparent and certainly more hopeful and optimistic towards future situations.

We all haul around baggage and unforgiven wrongs we have suffered. Some are small like the person that cut you off in traffic or the lack of a smile from the grocery store clerk. Others are quite big and traumatic in nature such as the grief associated with the loss of a loved one, the dissolution of a marriage, or the loss of a beloved job.

The cost and drain caused by unhealed and unforgiven baggage can be extensive. It affects our demeanor, it pulls at our emotional energy, and it often impacts the relationships we have with others. Unforgiven wrongs and unhealed grief will also impact our interpersonal skills. Often the people that are the gruffest with the least number of social skills are carrying a lot of baggage that is weighing them down. Unforgiven baggage and unhealed hurts also taint our view of people, situations, and the world around us. We automatically assume that more hurt will come because of the unresolved past situations. We expect it and that creates harm to our relationships and approaches to situations.

Unhealed hurts and unforgiven wrongs also produce snarky, sarcastic, and jaded responses from people. Some do it in a laughing or "fun" manner. These behaviors lead to a lack of forgiveness and healing. Another almost perverse sounding behavior common among the unhealed and those carrying unforgiven wrongs is that they will tend to hurt others. Intentional or not, they project their wrongs and hurt onto others. They hurt and carry pain, so they want others to do the same. I know this sounds odd and almost counterintuitive, nonetheless it happens more frequently than you may imagine. Never trust your tongue or your fingers and thumbs on keyboards, when you are unhealed and carrying unforgiven baggage.

An important note here is that some people just do not want to let go of their grudges and grief. They enjoy either the victimhood that comes with it or they have become accustomed to using grudges and grief to justify their current behaviors. It serves them well. They act like that because of the grief and unforgiven wrongs, and we often facilitate that and even encourage that crutch.

Another interesting dichotomy is that many of the people that seek and desire the forgiveness of others will often withhold that with their own past wrongs or perceived wrongs. They want forgiveness but fail to provide it. Or at least fail to provide real forgiveness.

Also, of importance to note is that there are fakers out there. Those that profess forgiveness but eagerly dredge up past wrongs in any interaction. They say they have forgiven you but define the current reality based on the past wrong. This is nowhere close to forgiveness. Likewise with grief and traumatic events, there are those who will claim healed status or near healed status yet cling to the grief and reminders of it constantly.

The levels of impact associated with unforgiven actions and unhealed grief varies with the event itself. There is little impact with brief anger about someone cutting you off in traffic. There is significant impact when the events rise to the level of trauma. As the severity of the wrong or hurt increases, so does the impact it has on our lives.

The definitions of forgiveness and healing are important to note at this point. Forgiveness is the solemn personal promise to not let the event impact future interactions or other forward progress. Forgiving is not forgetting and remembering past wrongs will keep you from repeating the same mistakes and defeating patterns. Forgiveness puts the event or issue far in the background so that no further harm to you or others occurs.

For our purposes, healing is the rebuilding of life and performance that needs to occur after a difficult situation or traumatic event. Healing is not the constant revisiting of the event or situation and returning to anger or grief, but it is the start of returning to normalcy in behavior and the needed step before forward progress can occur.

Our targeted shift to being healed and forgiven will create effortless interactions with others and eliminate those obstacles from building the life and achievements you desire. Forgiveness and healing take the mud off your heart and adds lightness and joy to your life.

The ability to move forward requires both healing and forgiveness. The desired outcome and mindset, belief, and attitude shift is into a world that is healed, forgiven for your sake, and all interactions come from a spot of good, or even great, emotional health.

True Forgiveness is a Gift to Yourself

The keys to reducing the drag of baggage and grief requires us to go through a process. Sometimes this process will be very quick and almost done in the background. In other cases, the process will take significant time and intentionality. In still other cases, the process is quite fluid and not linear, and they bounce around between grief and healed.

To improve healing and forgiveness, begin:

1. Feel the Feels
I know this sounds trite and to those of you experiencing genuine grief, it sounds downright insulting. This step is about acknowledging, admitting, and feeling the emotions associated with an event. It is perfectly alright and normal to be momentarily angry at the guy that cuts you off in traffic.

This does not mean that you stay stuck in those feelings for a long period of time or even in some extreme cases, indefinitely. It means that you acknowledge the feeling you have, not repress or deny them, and actively find a healthy way to express them or get them out.

It is perfectly fine to feel blue, cry, express a little anger, or be disappointed. Acknowledge this and then work to move forward.

2. Create Space to Grieve

Even the smallest setbacks need some time to grieve. If a valued team member leaves, take time to grieve the loss. If you lost a tennis match, take a moment to grieve it. This may seem odd on events that are less than human loss or relationship breakup, but we need to take this step to move forward, our goal.

Far too many people cope with loss, any loss, by jumping immediately into action or busyness. A parent dies and we immediately move into taking care of arrangements, caring for others, telling people the news, and just stirring around and not facing the grief. The same is true with smaller events too. We lose a valued team member, and we immediately launch into looking for their replacement, sometimes even before they have left the building. We need to make the space to grieve this loss, even if it is for a short period of time.

Grieving is a normal and natural human behavior. It is the experience of the emotion of loss (see above about Feeling the Feels) and the recollection of the great experiences and memories associated with whatever was lost. Again, like forgiveness, grieving is not about forgetting. It is about dealing with and accepting the changes associated with the loss and letting go of the emotions associated with that loss.

The failure to grieve often shows up in a job loss. Rather than creating a short time to grieve and recover, the newly unemployed jump right into a job search and associated interviews. Unfortunately, without the grieving and forgiveness needed, this emotional baggage will create a drag and harm the job searches and interviews. Similarly, people coming out of a breakup immediately pound the keyboard on internet dating sites without truly grieving the loss of their past relationship.

Tactically it is important to schedule the time to grieve. Make it a point to tell yourself, and even calendar, your grief time. This will vary based on the severity of whatever loss you are experiencing. For a mortal loss, this will take a while and should not be rushed. For smaller losses, this time can be as small as ten minutes. Whatever the time needed is, make it and don't compress it. It is also quite okay to adjust this time as needed and revisit the desire to heal later.

3.   Honor the Past but Don't Live There
It is totally cool, and even respectful, to honor the past and think fondly of it. These set of fond memories are part of the healing and moving forward journey. We should never repress or subordinate these.

Care should be taken in how much and how frequently recalling fond memories, creating memorials, and talking about the past is done. A general rule of thumb is to recall fondly but share that recall sparingly. If you have ever been around someone who talks endlessly about their old company and compares it to the new situation, you know how disconnecting this behavior can be. You will never fully connect with the present, and the people in it, if you are constantly reminiscing about the past. Likewise, the present and current will never fully accept you if you are chronically talking about and living in memories.

We must also be concerned with items that remind us of past events or long-gone people. If the items or trinkets or memorials bring fond memories, keep them around. If looking at them causes pain, and almost a return to grief, it would be best to remove them or at least store them away somewhere out of constant reminding sight.

4. Actively Forgive

Without being redundant, forgiveness is the promise to not let a past event, issue, or person impact all future interactions or situations. To practice forgiveness, we must be intentional and often speak the words, not to another person, but to ourselves to make forgiveness real and tangible.

It also becomes necessary to provide self-talk reminders of this forgiveness. When situations stir up memories of a hurt or wrong, we must immediately remind ourselves that this person or event has been forgiven and thus not allowing those negative feelings to creep into the current interaction or situation.

Forgiveness needs to be performed as close to immediately as possible. The only way to keep our baggage from overflowing and to ultimately unpack it, is to provide forgiveness. Most of us have met that bitter soul at work who somehow was wronged in 1997 and still carries that hurt around in all interactions today. Do not be that person. We have also met the wronged ex-spouse who divorced in 2010 and adds bitterness and jadedness to all encounters with other people. Forgiveness is the only cure for these pieces of baggage.

One piece of encouragement as you start practicing forgiveness more openly is to note, in journal-type form, three things that you need to forgive. It may include yourself for things you have done incorrectly or improperly in the past as well. Now set this list aside for a few days or even a week. Return to the list and add two or three more items and set it down again for another week. And one last time, look at the list again and soul search, or memory search, for any other baggage, hurt, or wrong, that needs forgiveness. Often with this additional time and self-examination, we find unforgiven issues and events that can go as far back as our childhood. Feel free to add to the list as something comes to mind.

Now the hard part begins when you note from your forgiveness list a date certain or deadline when you will provide that forgiveness. It does not have to be immediately, and you may need to do some grieving prior to granting forgiveness, so set a date that will be reasonable for you for you to forgive the event or person and finally release the drain and drag it has on you. Not a year from today, but a reasonable date ranging from tomorrow to in a few months. And it is on that date that you consciously and very intentionally forgive, promising not to let it influence the future or future interactions again. Not to forget, but truly forgive.

Not talking to someone or avoiding the situation that may have harmed you is not forgiveness. This is nothing more that denial (the famous river in Egypt). This is a compression of your baggage and nothing more. You can never fully recover by avoiding and denying situations. You must forgive completely, not avoid, to move forward.

Forgiveness of past wrongs and hurt is one of the most freeing and energizing things you can do for yourself and the people around you.

5.   Understand History as a Predictor
If history was truly a good predictor of future conditions, we humans would be living in total peace and harmony, skipping hand-in-hand on this beautiful blue marble that we occupy.

Unfortunately, history is not a good predictor, but people with unresolved and unhealed hurts and those carrying unforgiven wrongs will believe that all future conditions and interactions will be exactly as the one that caused them harm. History truly tells us nothing except for the reasonable certainty that tomorrow will come, and the sun will rise in the east. We can take those to the bank. Other than that, we need to treat every situation and every person as being unique and new. Shake your Etch-A-Sketch and clear the slate of history when looking at opportunities, changes, people, and situations. Nothing will occur the same and often trying it again will prove to be successful.

6. Give Thanks

One of the great healing process steps is to give thanks for what you do not have anymore. Be grateful for what was and celebrate the good you had with whatever changed or was lost. Again, do not stay stuck in the reminiscences, openly be appreciative of the good times, fun, success, adventures, and challenges overcome from the past situation or the lost person. When appreciation is added with forgiveness, it creates the most powerful emotional energy restoring possible.

You may even consider journalling, for a short and fixed, period of time, all of the appreciation of whatever it is that you lost.

7. Rediscover Yourself

Grieving, and even the granting of routine forgiveness, is a great time to rediscover who you are. Take inventory of the things you like to do, the situations you like to be in, and the people you enjoy being around. Identify what makes you happy, what creates points of personal satisfaction, and what grants you relief from the everyday grind. By identifying these, you will begin to craft your path forward out of loss and past forgiveness.

8. Craft a Path Forward

Even with the simplest and quickest piece of forgiveness granted, we must create a path forward, a determination for how the future will look. With deeper traumatic grief events, this becomes more detailed and more complicated.

We have to map, sometimes just mentally, what we are going to do, how we will respond (not react) in the future, who we want to surround ourselves with, and define the future condition. This step is extremely critical and becomes a self-promise, of sorts, and helps create a guiding path for our future beliefs and attitudes. This is also the commitment to stay in a state of forgiveness, not falling back into baggage, and remaining healed, and not returning to grief.

Abundance Replaces Scarcity Belief

"True abundance isn't based on net worth, it's based on our self-worth."
Gabrielle Berstein

Abundance is the belief, and knowledge, that we have everything we need or will have everything we need. It eliminates cravings, jealousy, and comparisons with what others have. It is a significant and powerful shift into living in a state of knowing you have everything needed and desire nothing else tangible. This belief of abundance, and the associated gratitude will create more of what you have.

The abundance mindset and belief also require us to accept things as perfect just as they are. So instead of "this is a great chair, but a leather recliner would sure be awesome", the shift is "this chair is great and perfect for my needs". We also need to make sure we do not add "but" phrases to our appreciation of what we have. Everything you have is what you need, and it is perfect exactly as it is.

Scarcity belief is the immediate assumption that you do not have enough. It is usually expressed in the form of money, time, or support. The danger in scarcity belief is that it will dramatically hinder any thoughts of growth that require significant investment. It also condemns us to being stuck where we are and doing what we are doing.

What it sounds like: "I do not have enough time for that"; "I do not have that kind of money"; "Maybe someday when we win the lottery", "I'll need a personal assistant to get that done"; "I'll do that when the timing is better".

Often this belief is generational and passes from father to son, mother to daughter. My parents were born during the Great Depression and had mastered the art of making President Roosevelt scream when he left their fingers. For years, I worked to overcome this belief that there was never enough, especially money.

You Have Everything You Need

Scarcity beliefs and attitudes drive comparisons, and even jealousy. In a world where the fakery of social media is constant, we often look at what others have, their happiness, their material wealth and trinkets, their homes, their families, and compare that to our genuine state or condition. Not only is that comparison apples and oranges, but it also creates an inherent want to be like them or have what they have. When unchecked, craving for what others have will cause jealousy. Jealousy is one of the most dangerous emotional states and causes a great deal of harm to your overall demeanor and how you interact with others. Jealousy will also consistently drag your emotional energy. Scarcity beliefs will also drive a lack of tolerance for even the modest risks.

The scarcity of time is also pervasive in many people. The claim that there is not enough time to get something done that they want to do. Not enough time to start school again. Not enough time to juggle all the demands that are on their plate currently. Not enough time to go the gym. The important shift here is to learn to prioritize what you really want to do and to create time from where you did not see it possible before.

Time scarcity also shows up in the readiness. Often people will express a desire to move ahead or to take on a new and exciting opportunity, but the time is just not right. There are still kids at home, work is very intense, I am just not in the right mood for that, blah, blah, blah. Opportunity waits for no one, and the timing will never be perfect. Learn to welcome the opportunities as they come and juggle the timing and other demands on you as you go along. It will work out just fine. We must make time for what we truly find important and want to do.

Another scarcity relates to people. Some people will express a lack of people in their life, a lack of friends, a lack of support systems. Not only is this scarcity not true, as we have more people in our life than we realize, but it can also generate a sense of loneliness and isolation. The curative piece of this is also obvious in that we have the ability to add people, good people, to our life at any time.

Like with all the belief limiters, these take more work over an extended time. Because beliefs are deeply rooted and formed over time, it will take focused work to get past this one.

Strategies for Overcoming Scarcity Belief:

1. Practice Gratitude

Please see the previous section about Failure to Appreciate to see the instructions for the practice of gratitude. To recap, note daily what you are thankful for, share some of those with other people, and continue this process. Gratitude is a powerful belief set that drives excellent results and behaviors in people.

2. Prioritize

There is a high likelihood that the resources exist that you need to achieve your dreams and goals. Equally likely is that some of those resources are being poorly allocated. If you want to return to school, the $12.00 vanilla soymilk latte could be better allocated to a savings account. The same with recreation, entertainment, and dining out money. Could you live with one car for a period? Could you stay in the apartment a few more months? Make your dream and goal the priority and ensure the money will follow. That flow of money is a true feature of an abundance attitude and belief set.

Similarly, prioritizing time towards what you want must be prioritized, even above areas of personal comfort, vanity, and self-pleasure. That time will always be available to you but should come after the time invested in needed priorities.

3. Outsource and Delegate

If time is really the issue and no amount of prioritizing will give you the needed time, outsource some of the things that consume your time. I am pretty good at cleaning. Not spectacular, but pretty good. But I also realize that my time accomplishing important things is far more valuable than the few hundred dollars spent on a housekeeper. The same with yard work, ironing my dress shirts, changing the truck's oil, and a few more. Compare the value of your time in that activity that prevents you from executing your desired outcomes. Outsource all that is reasonable and use that new time wisely.

4. Budget Carefully

Just as you would enter a budget line item for utilities, groceries, payments, and the like, create a budget line item to accumulate the money needed to achieve what you desire. Here is the catch: fund this line item first. Not when you have extra money. Not after the holidays. Not when you can. First. Before the house payment. Before groceries. First. Make your desires a living reality by setting aside what is needed as a priority.

5. Manage Your Circle

We need the help of others. It can sometimes be as simple as a change in schedule, modifying who picks up what kids and when, or agreeing to time blocks needed to study. Those others can include our family, a boss, or a group of friends.

Scarcity in support can be genuine or imagined. We never really know until we ask others for help in supporting our dreams. If that support is not forthcoming, we need to examine who we have allowed into our inner circle. If you are surrounded by non-supporters or naysayers, you need to remove them from your circle immediately. Keep the supporters, encouragers, and helpers close to you. You may have to make this adjustment multiple times. Grow you circle and people in your life as needed.

6. Inventory Resources
Often, the scarcity of resources is entirely imaginary. Start by taking account of what you have. The money, time, and support you can count on. You may be surprised, pleasantly so, at what you have available to you. Write it down and get it out of your head.

7. Seek Alternatives and Creative Solutions
This is especially prevalent with scarcity of money. Investigate creative solutions that may exist. Leave no stone uncovered related to grants, loans, matching funds, and the like. They are out there. My community has a little-known microloan program for new businesses. It is not a lot of money, but it is something that many people do not know about. Keep searching and leave no stone unturned.

8. DIY
Do it yourself. This thought sends chills down a great many people's backs especially when considering things like remodeling, a new backyard, or restoring a vehicle.

Thirty-some odd years ago, I was overwhelmed by the costs of starting and running a small business. The list of things I could not afford was much larger than the list of things I could afford. Stubbornly, I set out to do as much myself as I humanly could. Designed our first logo. Built our website. Designed program guides and handouts. They were admittedly not the best and much was replaced later by professionally done work, but it was a start. And it worked out nicely.

With a little determination, you can self-learn just about anything. Web pages, graphic design, marketing, whatever. You can learn it and get it going until you are at a place to have it outsourced and professionally done. The satisfaction associated with learning new things and doing something yourself is priceless as well.

9. Confront the Source
Is your scarcity belief real or imagined? Has it been generationally passed to you? Is it an easy excuse to use?

Those are tough questions but necessary to eliminate scarcity belief for good. Take some time and truly analyze these questions and confront where they originate. It may be hard to admit that you made it up, but that can also be extremely liberating in your pursuit of your dreams and expanding your beliefs and attitudes beyond what limits you now.

Positive Expectations Replace Pre-Condemned Outcomes

"Once you replace negative thoughts with positive ones, you'll start having positive results."
Willie Nelson

Creating expectations of great outcomes, and the optimism associated with that, will drive great results and a significant shift in your demeanor and behavioral projections. When we look forward to things, even small, everyday occurrences, it adds an energy that will drive your results and interactions with other people. This attitude and belief will have a significant impact on your behaviors. The expectation of a positive outcome is a furthering of the use and embracing of optimism. Ultimately, creating an attitude of positive expectation rallies your hope that something will be good, an interaction will be positive, and it ignores, quite purposefully, any history to the contrary. If forces us to look at every future event through the lens of possibility and hope, rather than pre-condemnation.

Some people must have some amazing crystal balls and the ability to look into the future. They make Madam Zorro at the county fair look like a damn amateur. They can forecast the upcoming meeting will be a waste of time. They can predict the date will not go well and they will not hit it off. They can look into the future and see they will not get the promotion. They can accurately (or so they believe) assess that the customer phone call will not go well. Amazing skill these people have.

Sadly, this isn't any kind of paranormal or psychic skill they are using. They are engaging in the dangerous, and also sadly, self-fulfilling expectation of a negative outcome. They look at a future activity and predict that it will not go well or will be a total waste of time and energy. This negative expectation drives common behaviors such as your facial expressions, the tone of your voice, and the words you choose. Other people will see this and that will often create the self-fulling nature of negative expectations. Others will feed from your behaviors driven by the negative expectation and what you were predicting will absolutely come true.

Not too long ago, I was scheduling a phone call with someone and from the tone of her text message, she was not looking forward to the conversation. Sure thing, her text tone affected my approach, and the call did not go well. Her projected expectation of a negative outcome created the actual outcome.

Here is another case where history and unforgiven wrongs do not serve us well. We use the history of the last occurrence as the true predictor of all future occurrences. To wit: he did it once, he will surely do it again. Unfortunately, this is just not the case, and we need to shake our Etch-A-Sketch once again. Just because something occurred before or a prior interaction with someone was not good does not mean that will repeat.

If You Believe It Will Be Good, It Will Be

When we craft a positive expectation, our facial expressions are better, our body language is more open and welcoming, the tone of our voice is better, the words we select are much better chosen, and we listen better. All terrific behaviors to have and maintain and all driven by that positive expectation.

We do have to make sure that our positive expectation is rooted in some reality and not a total fantasy. We cannot expect the job interview to result in them offering you a vice-presidency role, company car, and million dollar signing bonus. We cannot hope that first date ends in love at first sight (some do) and you ride off into the sunset together. What we can set for a positive expectation is that the interview will go well, and you will present yourself well. The date will go well, and you will be able to go out again. Our expectations should be positive and optimistic but not a fairytale. That will only result in your disappointment that the best possible scenario did not happen.

To craft expectations of a positive outcome, begin using the following:

1. Ignore the Past and History
That Etch-A-Sketch is getting a lot of work. We must intentionally put aside and ignore any history of a negative outcome. Just because the interview last week did not go well does not mean today's version won't go splendidly. History is not a good predictor, and it must be ignored.

2.   Define What You Want and the Desired Outcome
Take some time and define, or even note, what your desired outcome looks like. How will it flow? What are the desired agreements? What do you want from the interaction? Note all of those and lock them in your mind. Remember to stay rooted in reality and not create a fantasy set of desired outcomes.

3.   Set a Short-Term Intention
Intentions are powerful, usually single word, reminders that help guide us for a moment or longer. If you have ever mentally reminded yourself to remain calm or to smile or to stay composed, you have set an intention.

For our purposes here, our intention set will be a single word that describes our desired outcome for any event. Consider using words like agreement, satisfied, peaceful, engaged, movement, forward, growth, etc. When setting your intention, be sure to use the desired terms and not the absence of a negative term. When using the absence of a negative (I won't react), your mind and emotions often process the negative.

4. Connect to a Bigger Purpose
Not every situation will have a perfectly desired outcome, but we can connect situations to a bigger purpose or our "why". Even though the meeting may seem to be needless, it allows me to have the opportunity to build rapport with the key stakeholders of a bigger project or bigger purpose. Look at situations, and even people, as steps toward a greater purpose and greater good. Once you connect these dots, setting a positive expectation becomes easier.

5. Use Some Perspective

Negative expectations of outcomes are often crafted for such minor interactions and situations. So, what if the customer you are calling is a pain the ass. It will last three minutes, and it won't affect your long-term happiness or success. Put everything through the lens of long-term perspective and value.

Optimistic and Upbeat Replace Dour, Complaining, and Defeated

"Perpetual optimism is a force multiplier."
Colin Powell

Optimistic and upbeat people are magnets for more upbeat, positive and optimistic people. Your optimism and upbeat demeanor will attract many more of those types of people into your life. Additionally, consistent upbeat, positive and optimistic attitudes will have a very solid effect on your physical energy and health. Optimistic and upbeat people are happier, more successful and have wider and deeper relationships.

Optimism and being upbeat also has a significant impact on our physical energy. When we are happy, we have a bit more of a pep in our step, more of a desire to take things on, more get up and go. That cannot be underemphasized. We have more energy to everything that comes our way when we are vibing at the higher frequency of optimism and upbeat.

The impact of optimism and your upbeat demeanor on others around you is important to note too. When you are upbeat, that will influence, in a very positive way, the mood of others around you. Their bad day will get brighter from the light you are able to radiate. Your hopeful and optimistic view of life, and even challenges facing us will inspire others to have the same. Indeed, optimism is a force multiplier. You have the power to inspire others in a very positive way by embracing this attitude daily.

A little warning about upbeat and optimistic includes the overuse of either or both. Optimism and upbeat (happy) are powerful drivers of great behaviors and outcomes but not all situations and people will appreciate that approach. There are people who will call out the overly optimistic or happy which is a warning that the situation was wrong for it. Use great judgment and self-management when displaying your optimism and upbeat demeanor and add some pragmatism to how you view the world. Not all situations and people are great, and you cannot expect them to be. Be optimistic but keep your feet firmly planted on the grounds of reality.

That one cubicle curmudgeon, that horrible energy vampire, who has not had a good day since the mid-1990's is a great example of dour and defeated. The best he can summon is a grunt and seems to celebrate the fact that no one likes him, and no one bothers to include him in anything. An interesting note about this creature is that the only people drawn to him are other bitter, negative and complaining souls. Likewise, is the person who would complain about the taxes paid if they won a million dollars in the lottery. Their constant complaining and whining about everything will only draw more of that into their life. This has such a negative impact on their physical, mental, and emotional health. These people will suffer far more maladies than happy people, they will have significantly fewer connected relationships, they will struggle overcoming injury, and they will always be grinding to produce enough energy to just get through the day.

Thinking the Best of Other People Will Help Them be Their Best

Often the negative souls we encounter are carrying the weight of unhealed loss and unforgiven wrongs. Also common with these people is they lack the coping and self-management skills to recover from multiple wrongs and losses. When they start piling up, they get more bitter, more difficult, and dourer. When unchecked and unmanaged, this dourness, bitterness, and constant complaining can also lead to clinically diagnosed depression disorders.

The dour negative attitude owned by some will also be projected in their tone and over-reliance on sarcasm and snarky comments. No matter the situation, they can point out issues with it and always have a smartass remark for everything and everyone. These people need attitude adjustment (as in transplant) desperately.

The constant complainer, or even the frequent complainer, must find something wrong with anything. Their go to phrase always includes "but". The food was good, but the service was terrible. He was a great boyfriend, but he had some issues with being impulsive. Always something to complain about and always finding the dark cloud in the completely blue sky. Often these people display the behavior of hyper-criticality described earlier. This is such a drain on both the person complaining and all the people around them. This will keep people running from you for quite some time unless fixed.

To reach optimism and upbeat, and pull out of negativity, sourness, bitter, and nasty, start working on:

1. Practice Gratitude and Inventory Your Blessings
We will never intimate that the practice of gratitude is a magic wand that cures all ills, but it certainly is close. Refer to prior sections about how to practice gratitude. If you are truly a bitter soul, continue this for a long period of time and really put thought and work into your gratitude notations.

Also take time to look for the good and inventory your blessings. Those should include even seemingly small things like you are alive, you have a job to go to, you have food and shelter, you have people around you. When we look at the fundamental things that we often take for granted, we begin to see how blessed we truly are.

2. Practice Forgiveness
Forgiveness relieves your emotional energy and your heart from prior wrongs and many hurts. You must let go of all the past negativity before you can rebuild a solid base of positivity and optimism. Please see earlier sections for more on forgiveness and the power it brings you. If you are the bitter soul described above, you will have to spend some significant time identifying the past wrongs that bring your attitude down.

3.   Heal Old Wounds

As described earlier, the process of grieving and healing is important for any loss, and even more so with significant losses. Your lack of healing will drag you to bitterness very quickly and we must actively work to heal before we can embrace upbeat and optimistic.

4.   Create Positive Intentions

This step is incredibly important for a consistently positive and optimistic attitude and belief set. Create one word for each day that will be your anchor word. This word is your mantra for the day and should be a powerful reminder of our happiness and optimism. Examples can include love, hope, joy, happiness, peace, growth, etc. Choose your word thoughtfully and intentionally. It will be your guide for the day. Sometimes this becomes as simple as reframing simple things like the difference between having to go to work and getting to go to work.

5.   Surround Yourself with Upbeat and Optimistic Souls

Many times, when we are down or in a negative attitude space, more of the same comes to us. This is so incredibly counterproductive. Make sure your circle, especially the closest ones and the ones you listen to the most, display a consistently upbeat, positive, and optimistic approach. Nothing will challenge us more than being surrounded by the nasty and pessimistic. You may have to create distance with some people or even completely disconnect from them to ensure your attitude remains healthy.

6. Rebuff Negativity

When negativity and negative people come your way, and it and they will, rebuff it assertively. Tell others you don't want to hear gossip or bad things about others. Put the negative news story down. Walk away politely from the complainers. Don't validate excessive sarcasm and snark. Push back when negative comes your way, and you will build a reputation of not wanting to be around it and it will not come to you as much.

7. Watch Reactions and Desire

Other people give us instant and constant feedback about our attitude, and we need to tune into and pay attention to these signals. Do go out of their way to connect with you, work to make time to talk with you, or do they avoid interacting with you? Do they sound excited and smile (more on this one shortly) when you connect with you or do they appear pensive and even defensive? These reactions will tell you everything you need to know about the attitude you are projecting.

8. Smile

I don't care about your dental work or even any cultural norms for smiling. A smile is a highly endearing expression that projects a positive attitude. It is the ultimate magnet for people and is very welcoming and approachable. Practice smiling in almost all your interactions with others and even when you are alone. It is a great reminder of the attitude we want to embrace.

9. Set Positive Expectations

When we set positive expectations for outcomes in all interactions and situations, this becomes a great reminder of the attitude we need to display. Conversely, when we set a negative expectation, our attitude and behaviors follow the lead of that expectation. Expectations, when set realistically, will become the reality for the situation. Choose a positive expectation and your attitude will flow with that.

10. Establish Goals and Find Purpose

Often the bitter, nasty, and snarky people we encounter are spending significant time on the hamster wheel of life. Working and moving but getting nowhere. They put in the time and effort but have nothing to show for it and haven't really grown or made significant headway for quite some time. This also occurs when people are checking off the calendar days as they near retirement. No goals, no purpose, just surviving day-to-day.

The easiest cure for the lack of direction attitude drag is to set some short-term and long-term goals for yourself. They can be professional or personal, relate to your health and wellness, be about learning new things, or even about getting out and meeting new people. Set some goals, track the progress regularly or daily. You must focus your efforts on those things that set your soul afire.

About a year and a half ago, I set a goal related to pushups and tracked my progress religiously, even annoyingly sharing it with people occasionally and posting it on social media. On my first day, I did 10 pushups. Shortly after I did 25. Within six months, I was consistently doing 1000 a month. Earlier this year I hit a streak of three consecutive months with over 2000 pushups. The goals drove my positive and optimistic attitude, and my attitude drove my behavior of doing pushups. The tracking and hitting of smaller incremental goals along the way continued to fuel my attitude in a very powerful way. Likewise, you will experience a new positive and optimistic direction with goals, tracking them, and celebrating the milestones along the way.

As with goals, discovering your purpose has a very positive impact on your attitude. Take some time to discover your "why". Why are you on the planet? What impact do you want to leave behind? How do you want to be remembered? Is there a legacy project that you want to accomplish? All those questions are about discovering your purpose. Find it and allow it to be your daily guiding light but comparing all your actions and your projected attitude to this purpose. Find your "why".

People and Experience Legacy Replaces Shallow Consumerism and Self-Worship

"People will forget what you said, forget what you did, but people will never forget how you made them feel."
Maya Angelou

Dr. Kenny Guinn was the former governor of the State of Nevada, Superintendent of Schools for Clark County, President of UNLV and a widely recognized business leader in banking and utilities. There are buildings named after him in Southern Nevada and there are even some statues of him around town. Almost every year, there was some type of dinner or gala in his honor, sometimes several. He was also my former boss.

As impressive as all his philanthropy, community involvement and leadership are, that is not Dr. Guinn's legacy or lasting memory. What I remember about Dr. Guinn is when in encouraged me with a funny story down in the parking lot. I remember when he was governor, he took time to take a picture with me and my oldest son. I remember his demeanor and approachability at work and his humility in meetings. I especially remember when I ran into him at the Reno airport, and we spent 30 minutes or more catching up. He asked about me and my kids and how work was going. This was his legacy to me. Not the buildings. Not the memorials. Not the statues.

197

And I am not alone. I have heard stories like mine dozens if not hundreds of times over the years. He was beloved by thousands. Admired not for the what but for the who he was and how he treated people. He built his legacy on what was important, the hearts of people. Helping them, making them feel important, valuing people. That will always be his legacy.

Conversely, I am aware of a hugely successful personal injury lawyer that absolutely has everything. Mansion, collection of exotic cars, expensive suits, beautiful wife, all the trappings of success. And he treats everyone he encounters, including that beautiful wife, like dog shit. He is a miserable person and treats people in rude and demeaning ways. He has crafted his legacy as well and it has nothing to do with success or good lawyering.

Unfortunately, I have bad news for you at this point. Your 401K balance, nifty new car, big house in the gated community, and all the other material things you have accumulated won't be coming with you in the afterlife. And chances are that after the inheritance is spent, your memory will become fleeting with those who were in your last will and testament. A few other things that won't last or appear on your headstone is all of your cool awards, your educational achievements, and those pictures of you donating to good causes. What is going to last, however, is how you choose to treat people and how they choose to remember you. The great news is that all this legacy is your choice, and you can carve it on solid ground beginning now.

Beginning in the post-World War II America, we devolved into a consumerist and materialism society in which we felt compelled to accumulate things and tie our self-esteem based on what we have and the recognitions we received. It has become all about acquiring more and more, achieving more and more, being envious when we don't have what the neighbors have, and even being resentful and jealous when we don't have what others have.

Consumerism and materialism create a vicious cycle of always needing more. Now, instead of the house on the hill, you need the house on the hill on the golf course in a gated community. The SUV no longer does the trick, and you now need a premium ride. Instead of going on vacation, you now need to have the mountain cabin or the beach house. All the while you are continuing to work harder and harder to provide more things. And as you work harder, your relationships deteriorate, you have less time for people, you treat others more abruptly and perhaps even rudely, your health suffers, you have less time to enjoy your things, and you may even find yourself as an earlier than predicted occupant of a coffin. But by God, we will certainly remember your things and your wealth.

Create Your Legacy on How You Treat People, Not What You Have Accumulated

The incredible saturation of social media into our everyday lives has certainly contributed to this as well. Now, we go no farther than our phones to see the perfect families, the major awards, and all the new cars. This has fast-tracked comparisons, envy and jealousy faster than seems possible.

We see the friend that has it, and we want it or are jealous they have it.

The attitude and belief shift here is closely related to the belief of abundance, but this is more about being happy with what we have and learning to value the truly important things. It will also be about crafting a legacy that is both inspiring and long-lasting. We need to shift our proposition of value from the material into how people feel and think of us. We need to shift from accumulation and selfishness into one of generosity, especially of time, and how we treat fellow humans. This shift will also be built on modesty and not showing off endlessly.

This is not about the Gandhi-esque selling of all you have and living on the streets in poverty. It is not at all about a vow of poverty, but it is about living within your means, enjoying the journey, having time for others, building deep relationships, and constructing (sometime requiring deconstruction first) a legacy built on your kindness, consideration, and how you valued people.

The other legacy shift here involves experiences and not about things. This is about taking every opportunity possible to explore new things, feel new feels, and see as much as you can possibly take in. This doesn't mean you have to go on a safari, backpack the Great Divide, or go dogsled racing, but it does mean that as opportunities for new experiences and meeting new people arise, you take them. You accumulate all those experiences and interactions, not shoes and suits. Add friends, true deep connections, and not boats and motorcycles. Those toys won't remember you but the people you touch certainly will.

To start the shift to a new and more powerful legacy, begin working on the following:

1. Inventory the Important
Take a few moments and think about, then note, what is truly important to you and how you want to be remembered. Write your own epithet and obituary both from the perspective of now and how you want to be remembered. What do you want people to say about you when you are gone? Note some keys you want them to remember, and this will also be part of an action plan to get there.

2. Explore and Expand
At every opportunity reasonably possible, explore the new. This does not have to be elaborate, but it can be trying new food, taking a new route home, walking the neighborhood, window shopping, trying a new hobby, or taking a short road trip.

Likewise with people, take every opportunity to meet new folk, and certainly to build deeper relationships with those you know. It's great that you have 2,000 Facebook friends but when you can't count even a couple of people in which you have true emotional intimacy and vulnerable trust with, those followers mean nothing. Build some, not a ton, of close relationships in which you can share anything, everything, successes, failures, emotions, feelings, attitudes, beliefs, and everything that is you and them. These are the relationships, not Facebook friends, that matter and will perpetuate your legacy.

3. Value People and Not Accomplishments

Although it sounds highly Machiavellian, and it is, there are those people who only value others for what they can do for them or have done for them and not for the whole person that they are. Legitimately value, by showing interest, inquiring (asking about them, their day, and things important to them), listening to, and being kind to, everyone you encounter. Build a reputation as the nice person, the one that others look forward to interacting with and not the one that always needs something or wants something. Value the person and not what they can do or have done for you.

4. Slow Down Achieving and Earning

The trap of acquiring stuff requires a lot of work. If you look at those in accumulation mode, you will find a lot of workaholics. Really kind of sad when you think about it. They want more so they must work harder (certainly not smarter) to get it. They have to be bigger to fuel bigger and bigger acquisitions of things. The first step here is to slow that down and reallocate that time to being with people and exploring the new. You can say no and only you can say no to the extra work. Your workaholism won't be a headline on your grave marker.

5. Give Without Recognition

Generosity is a hallmark of those who are well thought of by others but giving has some caveats to have the impact on our legacy desired. When we give, we must do so without any belief of a benefit coming to us or without any fanfare or recognition for doing so. Be quietly generous. You don't need to be feted at the banquet or receive a big plaque, just give what you can and when you can. Give a little extra on tips, hand the homeless dude a $20.00 (regardless of what he will do with it), put cash in the offering plate, and just be invisibly generous. This is great for your heart and emotional health and ensures your legacy will include your generosity.

6. Stop Comparisons
Comparing yourself to others, especially what you only see superficially, or on social media, is destined to create envy and jealousy. When you practice gratitude, are thankful for what you have, and create a belief of abundance, comparisons will mean nothing to you. Congratulate others for their success and accumulation of new things but stop wanting, craving, and coveting what they have. You don't know the price they paid for those things and don't know what is happening behind the curtains of Facebook. Celebrate your unique blessings and always be thankful for the important things like your health, family, relationships in your life, and how you contributed to someone else's happiness. Those have no comparison.

7. Reduce Judgements
Judgmentalism drives comparisons. Reduce and cease your judgements on others and change your standards for how success is measured. Rather than looking at the big house, nice car, and all the toys as being successful, look at happiness, peace, reputation, helping others, providing a great example, and contentment as the measure of success. It certainly is the lasting measure of success and how your legacy should be built.

8. Mentor Not Employ or Use

Spending time with people can take many forms. One of the most rewarding, for everyone involved, is to mentor people and not just employ them. Take the time to show interest in their development and their needs. Help them grow. Help them achieve their dreams and goals. Be their encourager. Be there for them when things don't work particularly well.

Dr. Abraham Maslow, the father of motivational science and the author of the motivational hierarchy, defined a level of motivation higher than self-actualization. He identified transcendence as the state of helping others achieve self-actualization. So from your perspective, when you mentor and grow others into meaningful success, you have achieved the highest state of motivation for yourself.

9. Forgive the Flaws

Instead of complaining endlessly and sharing your woes with others, forgive failures and lapses quickly. People are not perfect. Companies and organizations are not perfect. Forgive the wrongs and let it go.

Confidence and Humility Replaces Arrogance and Self-Centeredness

"Humility is not thinking less of yourself, it's thinking of yourself less."
C. S. Lewis

"A humble person is more likely to be self-confident, a person with real humility knows how much they are loved."
Cornelius Plantinga

Esteem extremes. Say that three times fast. It's fun to say, isn't it. Esteem extremes. Esteem extremes. Esteem extremes.

Occupying the far ends of the self-esteem and confidence equation, the very low and the very high. Everything in the middle of that, 80% of our self-esteem, is healthy and exactly where it should be.

First, let's start with the low extreme of self-esteem that drives low confidence. This is the individual that does not think very highly of themselves or their capability. This can be driven by a variety of emotional and psychological factors including childhood trauma, constant exposure to criticism or a critical environment, or lack of meaningful support and encouragement systems. The core of this extreme is a lack of belief in self and lack of seeing oneself in a positive way, or a consistently positive way.

The risks of unmanaged super-low self-esteem are many with a lack initiative and drive being in the forefront. Low self-esteem and the associated confidence will not attract people, there will be no desire to experience new things, and there will be no vision for the future or desire to discover a life's purpose. Low confidence and self-esteem may also be a signal that unforgiven wrongs and unhealed wounds are being carried around.

The other end of the extreme scale is also dangerous. Super-high self-esteem will produce arrogance, aloofness, self-centeredness, and a set of unapproachable and unrelatable behaviors. The overly self-valued will never be able to have self-awareness and never accept feedback from other people other than praise and adoration.

Confidence and humility are usually not included in the same sentence, much less linked as an important belief and attitude set. We often tend to look at these two as being mutually exclusive; you can have one, but not the other. Unfortunately, that view, largely fueled by images presented to us through the media. We can thank Muhammad Ali for beginning this trend.

Speak Less and Do More

True confidence is a quiet commodity. It is the self-assurance that you will, not can, deal with everything that comes your way. It is not a sense of perfection but rather a belief in being resolute and strong in everything you do. It is not a boisterous bravado but steely determination to get it done. Confidence drives action and results. Confidence inspires others and becomes a magnet for people as they want to follow those who project confidence. Confidence is silent while arrogance is quite loud.

Confidence drives our ability to explore the new, take on challenges, meet new people, and become vulnerable in relationships. It is the self-belief that we have what we need, and we are certainly good enough for all situations and people. Ultimately, our confidence is driven by how we see ourselves, our self-esteem. If we feel good about ourselves and who we are and what we have done, we will easily generate confidence.

Humility is quiet just like true confidence. Being humble is an approach that keeps you approachable and relatable to others, no matter what you have done and achieved in life. Humility is not weak, but rather an attitude rooted in the pure confidence that you don't need to boast or be the constant center of attention. When combined with confidence, humility makes you an extremely desired person to be around. Humility is open to share challenges along the way and not afraid to admit mistakes or apologize when needed.

One great indicator of a humble, and confident, approach is how they treat other people and specifically those who can't do one damn thing for them. They are nice to the dry-cleaning lady, they are polite and calm with the Wendy's drive through man, they respect all people, dismiss none, and use the same set of skills on the seemingly unimportant as they would with the important. Another indicative element of humility is the use of courtesy in all interactions no matter how big or small. They say please, thank you, excuse me, and I'm sorry frequently and with all people. In some respects, courtesy is the superpower behavior of the humble and confident. Courtesy and politeness are not weak, it is driven from a great inner strength and self-worth.

As much as confidence and humility draw people to you, arrogance and self-centeredness will push them away quickly. No one wants to be around the constant bragger and show off. Arrogance is an exaggerated view of yourself, your accomplishments, and your value to others. It is that attitude that often destroys people skills, and these arrogant souls will never show any interest in others. The arrogant will never have deep connections with others and often count multiple friends without having any of depth and vulnerable connection. Conversely, confidence and humility will drive great people interaction skills and relationships.

More bad news for you. I've been in the bathroom after you and guess what? Your shit does stink just like everyone else's. You're not perfect, your life is not charmed, everything you touch does not turn to gold, and we are not that interested in hearing about all your splendid exploits. Good for you but we don't care.

Self-centeredness is a bit different but related to arrogance. It is the belief that everything, conversations, interactions, meetings, and social media posts are about you. In its extreme, self-centeredness can drive paranoia and produce a very selfish approach to all situations. The self-centered don't share, whether it is the spotlight, credit, or Thanksgiving mashed potatoes. They truly think everything is for them and about them.

The self-centered attitude and belief can also drive some very rash and impulsive behaviors. They set an unrealistic expectation for communication responses and often lash out if those expectations are not me. The self-centered will also believe that every negative event, challenge, or issue is happening only to them and because of them. The office changed the hours just to punish the one self-centered soul. The self-centered is the only one that has hardships related to a sinking economy.

Self-centeredness will also create a heightened sensitivity about what others think of them. They will guard what others see and know about them at all costs and often become unreasonable when their projected illusion becomes challenged. They will actively solicit information about how others view them and manage large aspects of their life based on this. Everything they do must be in support of the self-centered image and reputation they have crafted. Self-centeredness as an attitude and belief sometimes becomes combined with hyper-sensitivity in this scenario.

As we move away from arrogance and self-centered into genuine confidence and humility, work on the following:

1. Manage Your Self-Talk
We all have a little voice in our head that gives us clues and signals about how to behave and where our attitudes and beliefs are at. It is imperative that we manage this voice and not become victim to it. Make sure your self-talk is consistently positive and encouraging. If it goes dark or

negative, we must intentionally and consciously redirect it back to the positive.

Use your self-talk to remind yourself about your great skills, attributes, and traits. This is not about using affirmations in the mirror, but rather a more powerful and consistent approach to the messages you feed yourself. Keep that little voice as your primary cheerleader and supporter.

2. Watch Your Pronouns
The overuse of first-person pronouns, I, me, I'm, I'd, mine, tend to be great indicators of too much self-worth and arrogance. Use plural pronouns when describing situations and events and certainly when talking about an achievement. If you think about it, you have really achieved nothing alone. You have had help, encouragement, and support along the way. Acknowledge it when the opportunity arises.

3. Just Say Thank You
The arrogant loves to share additional information when offered some praise or appreciation. Just say thank you and avoid spewing all the details of how you did it and the miraculous and heroic steps you took to get something done.

4. Be Polite and Courteous
Please, thank you, and excuse me matter a lot. People notice when you use them and certainly notice when you don't. When you build your reputation and memory points with others on being polite and the "nice person" that is a confident and humble base for your legacy.

5. Apologize

Own your mistakes and issues and trust that others will offer true forgiveness when your behavior also changes accordingly. Struggling with accountability and apologies is a surefire sign of arrogance. The confident and humble will apologize openly and quickly without any additional blame or justification coming along for the ride. When you have done something wrong or treated someone poorly, apologize. Use the first-person form of an apology by saying "I'm sorry" or "I'm truly sorry" or I'm sincerely sorry". Those are much more powerful and more meaningful than "I apologize". That statement comes across cold and without meaning. Even when wrong is shared or you are not the major contributor to an issue, apologize for your part in it. Again, this is strong and confident, and certainly not weak or shallow.

6. Share

Openly share and give what you have. Share the credit, share the spotlight, share the success, share the secrets of your successes, and share your history and story. Be open and transparent about who you are and how you got to where you are. Share the tangible as well. Pass the gravy.

A special note to my self-employed, entrepreneurial, and public official friends: Your sharing, and in some cases what some would consider oversharing, is necessary for your brand management. Like it or not, you are the face of your organization, and therefore the brand, and you must keep a positive profile in social media and other outlets.

7. Avoid Over-Sharing

But you don't need to share everything. Every time you go to a nice restaurant, go to the movies, or go out dancing, doesn't have to be a social media post. Church attendance and feeding the homeless looks a lot more like showing off than something noteworthy. It's certainly awesome that you have political beliefs, but kindly keep them to yourself. These things are nothing more than arrogant attention seeking. Of the billions of political statements and memes shared daily, not even one changes an opposing viewpoint, so maybe don't share them. Draw attention to yourself when it is noteworthy and be careful about the line that separates important and what is just showing off. If you think about it, many of the people we admire the most (not envy), share just enough to let the world know they are doing well and still alive.

Take the pictures, record the events, save the memories but either keep them for your own entertainment and enjoyment or share them with only a close circle of family and friends.

8. Compliment and Appreciate Others

One of life's greatest treasures and mysteries is the feeling WE get when we compliment and appreciate others and their actions. When we praise and compliment others, they feel great, and we feel restored and refreshed. Share some compliments freely and openly and spread appreciation whenever and wherever and to whomever possible.

9. Remember Past Successes

When you feel your confidence waning a bit, remember some of your past successes or periods of your life when you were particularly happy. Don't live there or even campout there but remember for the purpose of restoring your confidence. Some little reminders, like certificates, pictures, or trophies or the like, not a shrine or memorial garden, can help you remember and recollect these times of higher confidence.

10. Inventory Your Strengths

Take some time and identify the things that you are good at. Strangely, a lot of people struggle with this but the arrogant do not. The truly humble will not be good at this but it is an important restorative step if you feel your confidence falling a bit. There will be more about this and striking a proportion between what we have to work on and what we are good at later in this book.

11. Shift Gears

One strategy that helps both confidence and humility simultaneously is moving from one area of focus to another. The humility comes from the admission that you are struggling in a certain area or with another person. Confidence returns from the performance and success in the new area. So, if you are hitting your head against the wall working on the department's budget, set it aside for a bit, and focus on coaching some team members and providing them with some feedback. You may be struggling with one of your kids, disengage from them for a short period, and work in the back yard. This focus shift allows you to experience the successes, accomplishments, and milestones needed to restore your confidence to the needed levels.

Resilience Replaces Hypersensitivity

"Success is not final, failure is not fatal, it is the courage to continue that counts."
Winston Churchill

Since I already summoned the image of an arcane toy, I thought I would do it again. When I was a child, I always wanted one of those blow-up clowns with the big red nose and his base was filled with sand or cement mix or something that created his buoyancy. The object of this toy was to punch it, and it would immediately pop back up to repeat the boxing match.

Now before you are tempted to either feel sorry for me for not getting this toy, or buy one and send it to me, I have received several of varying sizes in my adulthood.

The point of the clown story is to illustrate what resilience is. Resilience is our ability to bounce back quickly from situations and return to normalcy in life and our professional performance. Like with forgiveness, it is not forgetting the obstacle but rather the promise that it will not influence us moving forward beyond the lessons learned.

The one promise I can make to you with absolute certainty is that you will face obstacles, challenges, and roadblocks of varying sizes and severity during your life. No one succeeds without bouncing back from and overcoming obstacles. No one has a perfectly charmed life and just about the time you do, issues will pop up in response to challenge to the universe. As we discussed legacy before, no one will remember the challenges you faced but they will remember how, and with what amount of grace, you responded to them.

Resilience will also grow into the persistence that is needed in many situations. Resilient people will persevere and work through almost all obstacles. Not in a blunt force kind of way, but rather in a methodical, "I'm not going to give up", and smart manner. Persistence is a very valuable behavior that is driven by our resilience in overcoming obstacles and challenges.

A lack of resilience, and in some cases hypersensitivity, shows up in some interesting behaviors. The easiest to visualize is the person that has a complete meltdown and shutdown when faced with an obstacle or challenge. They melt. They cry.

They become angry. They even become enraged. Another behavioral symptom is the "cut and run". You see this in job settings and in relationships. At the first sign of a challenge, those lacking resilience bail out, leave, and close the door, rather than working through the issues or challenges. To them it is easier to escape than it is to work through things. Unfortunately, this catches up with them quickly.

Another sign of lack of resilience was referenced in the prior sections about grief. Some people move into busyness mode rather than deal with the issues at hand that may require some soul searching, grieving, or forgiveness. They just get busy, and the problem is kicked down the road. This steely coldness is not a sign of good resilience and emotional intelligence. Quite the opposite as emotional intelligence is the acknowledgement of emotions and the appropriate use and regulation of the same.

Hypersensitivity contains elements of both over-rigidity in beliefs and self-centeredness in beliefs and attitudes. Hypersensitivity is an exaggerated, overly emotional, or completely inappropriate response to any scenario, or words spoken. Like with a lack of resilience, the reactions include shutting down, overly emotional including anger, sadness, and despair, and withdrawing. They hypersensitive seem to be offended by everything and anything. They see something that challenges their view of the world, and they immediately have a meltdown. One other common element of the hypersensitive is that they are never content in keeping what wronged or offended them to themselves, they must broadcast their rage and hurt widely. This is where the connection to self-centeredness comes in and it also shows up when the hypersensitive person believes everything is a slight or pokes at them.

Not Everything is About You

A lack of resilience and adoption of hypersensitivity will have a significant impact on your confidence and will also impact your ability to be open and flexible. Emotional outbursts and withdrawing behaviors (lack of people skills) are the hallmark of this belief set and attitude.

Here is a final note to the hypersensitive souls reading this: everyone you dislike is not a narcissist (diagnosed by amateurs after reading two internet articles about the same), everything difficult, unpleasant, or challenging is not trauma, everything spoken from ignorance is not racism, disagreements are not bullying or gaslighting, having your sensibilities or dogmas challenged is not being triggered, and conflict is not abuse. I know this sounds a bit harsh and overly direct, but we need to remember that single events do not deserve the common labels of the hyper-sensitive. We need to get some skin thickness and show some grace when confronted by life's everyday events. Upping your resilience will take care of these nicely.

One warning note about resilience is that if overdone and not balanced with healthy vulnerability and transparency, it can become aloof or even arrogant. That totally bulletproof, unaffected by anything or anyone has extended resilience beyond what is desired, and that person probably invest way too much time in self-care.

The resilient believe that every challenge is temporary, and it is only a matter of time and effort to overcome the issue. Resilience has true lasting power and will serve you well professionally and personally.

To shift into greater levels of resilience, work on:

1. Gain Perspective

Put the issue or challenge into genuine perspective. No, you didn't get the promotion, but you still have a great job and are still a highly thought of team member. You've crafted a great life with what you have. Yes, the Facebook comment bothered you and even a couple of your friends noticed it, but it was a minor blip on the radar screen of your image and reputation. Place all the events in the context of the largest scale possible to minimize the feeling of impact of those challenges.

2. Grow Confidence

Resilience and confidence are closely related and linked. Those with healthy confidence tend to have greater resilience. Those with good resilience will tend to have good confidence. When you openly work to grow and maintain your confidence by remembering past successes, shift focus as needed, identify your unique strengths and talents, and ensure your self-talk is positive, you will also be growing your resilience.

3. Take Care of Your Physical Body

Our resilience has both an emotional side and a physical side and they are closely connected. When we are tired, not in great shape, lack physical energy, or are ill or hurting, it is hard for us to be resilient. Pay attention to your diet, exercise, movement, and rest. All of those, when done in proportion and regularly, will greatly enhance your ability to be resilient and reduce any hypersensitivity.

4. Lean on Your Support Team

When you are feeling a little down, more sensitive than normal, and maybe lacking the resilience that you need, this is the time to lean on your inner circle. Be transparent and vulnerable and tell them that you are dragging. Let them work their magic and remind you of the terrific human that you are. Sometimes we all need a little reassurance, and you would certainly do that for them. Ask for their time and be sure to be willing to reciprocate when they need you.

Productive and Peaceful Replaces Busyness

"It is not enough to be busy. So are the ants. The question is: What are we busy about?"
Henry David Thoreau

"The essential question is not 'how busy are you?' but 'what are you busy at?'"
Oprah Winfrey

We must learn to balance our extremely limited time between being truly productive and being at rest. Our efforts and focus must be placed on what has meaningful value and not just being busy for the sake of being busy. Our belief and attitude shifts are to treat time as an investment and to use that resource on what is important and to change our view of rest and downtime into being as important as any achievement. We must shift into the importance of just being and not on being busy.

When I first became a father, my mom told me and the boy's mom that they will never remember how clean the house is, but they will always remember how much time you spend playing with, reading to, and just being around them. And it was true. Neither boy could even describe the house conditions, but they sure can recall times spent together fondly. The productive use of time here was making a positive impression on a young child.

Often our lives are frittered away being busy but without any connection to the important things. One of the most counterproductive attitudes and beliefs is the need to be perpetually busy. Be a blur, constant motion, always flitting from spot to spot. Never exactly sure what they are doing but by goodness they are busy. Busyness for some has become an addiction, no less engrained than how we think of traditional addictions. They have to be busy. They have to be doing something. They define themselves in terms of how busy, and in some cases, how stretched thin they are.

These super-busy souls are often trying to overcompensate for something or comparing themselves to other people. My brother is busy and a workaholic so I must copy that behavior to curry his favor. My spouse is always complaining about how busy he or she is so I must emulate that and be busy all the time as well. Busyness can trigger some unattractive behaviors related to people skills and even burn out the person addicted to busyness.

The need to be busy constantly can also morph into an addiction to stimulation. This is when a person is claiming to have down time but just sitting there and playing a game on their phone, checking for new messages, doom scrolling Facebook, watching a movie, or listening to music. Down time must be just that, a complete turnoff of the world.

A final note about the busyness attitude and belief and that is that they often need, if not crave, being around people. They despise being alone and must have someone with them constantly. These people also bounce from relationship to relationship without ever experiencing the needed alone time and independence.

Busy is Not a Coping Mechanism. Busy is Only Useful if it Serves a Greater Purpose

One of the things we must become comfortable with and even look forward to, is just being. Not with anyone, unless they are in just being mode too, not with background music, not with the television on for noise, but just being. You, alone with your thoughts and prayers, and maybe some meditation. This stillness is an incredibly important and healthy part of you and your self-care.

To eliminate our drive to be busy constantly and achieve more peace in our lives, begin working on:

1. Carve Out Being Time
Find time in your day to have some absolute down time to just be and meditate. This may require you to find an isolated place in your house or close your office door. It will also require you to silence your cell phone (yikes and gasp) and set it aside. No music, no television, just you and your thoughts. You will want to tell the key people around you what you are doing and make sure they respect this boundary. You may also have to get up earlier to stay up a bit later to make this happen. This is not about hours, find 15 minutes every day for this practice.

When you may be experiencing a poor stress reaction or feeling an anxious about something, do this prescriptively. Taking a little time to compose your thoughts and emotions will be a great investment of your time.

2. Be Comfortable with Your Own Company
Loneliness is a thing, and we do not want to discount that, and we humans are wired to have social connectivity and relationships. We never want to produce isolation or any feelings of loneliness, but you must develop a comfort for being alone, fully alone. Only you and your thoughts. Again, not for long, but for a bit.

3. Set Goals, Vision, and Purpose
The creation of goals and the discovery of your purpose is important for many reasons but here it allows us to focus our efforts on meaningful things and not just being busy. When we discover our purpose and set goals, we can connect our daily activities, tasks, and projects to those. When they do not connect, do not do them. See previous sections about both goal setting and purpose.

4. Prioritize
This is another item that was presented in previous sections but look at what you are doing (being busy at) and see what priority it has. Yes, maybe it does have to be done, but not now and not in the sacrifice of more important things. This is going to require you to identify what is genuinely important and connected to your core values as a person.

5. Ignore and Outsource

Like with the perfectionist having to ignore some little things (gasp again), the person with the busyness belief and attitude will have to forgo some things and outsource others. If it does not connect nicely to your goals and purpose or if there are more important things that need to be done, ignore it or give it someone else to do.

Delegation, even to our kids, can be a powerful tool to help us here.

Excellence (Not Perfection) Replaces Good Enough

"Many people can reach for and attain excellence. To do so consistently is what separates masters and geniuses from everyone else."
Paul Russo

Shifting from checking the box and saying something is done to really providing excellence and value is great way to ensure your legacy and build a solid reputation. It is not enough to simply do something; we must do it with the highest standard of excellence possible without crossing into perfectionism.

With as much as we all have going on, it is no wonder that we look at everything like a race against the clock. Every task, every project, every meeting, everything that comes our way has time sensitivity and deadlines. We must get things done. And indeed, we do.

Good enough, pronounced goodnuff, has become pervasive. We do just the minimum amount to label something as done. We don't double-check anything. We rush through it with barely enough time to hit the deadline and then immediately move on to the next time sensitive matter. This is actually very poor time management, as the time needed to fix something far outweighs any time saved by rushing, and it creates an impression of you that you are always rushed and more interested in staying busy.

My youngest son helped me install a couple of side yard gates for my girlfriend last year. A good-sized project that I had mapped out and knew what I wanted. Because of his experience in home improvement work and construction, I let him take the lead. And by God, we got it done in one Saturday. Record pacing. The problem is the workmanship makes me cringe. Joints not completely aligned, angles not perfect, and hinges not holding well. Certainly goodnuff. But not quality work at all.

Good Enough is the Enemy of Excellent

We must shift our attitude and belief from being deadline and time driven to more focused upon quality. Deadlines are important, and certainly must be met, but there is no reason we should slop through work just to hit a date and time. Commit to producing only excellence and quality in all facets of your life.

Similarly to tasks and projects, we often rush through interactions with others to move on to the next one or to return back to our time sensitive tasks. We must also commit to an attitude of excellence in our interactions with others. Provide them with the value other people want and the time that they certainly deserve.

1. Slow Down

Rushing through things doesn't make hitting the deadline any easier. In fact, you will end up making mistakes and producing poor work. Slow down, use a methodical pace, and really focus on what you are doing, not just rush. Move quickly, but with focused purpose and a commitment to excellence.

2. Focus

Multitasking does not work and is a great myth. Your brain (and mine too) is capable of singular focus on anything important. Quit trying to juggle multiple things and one time and eliminate all the distractions you can. Put down your phone, close your door, stop jumping at the new email that showed up, and truly focus on one thing at a time. The secret is not to do multiple things at once but to transition quickly between things you are working on.

Another aspect of focus is concentrating your mind solely on the task at hand and not letting your mind wander into all the other things you must do. This mindful approach is about being present in the current function or task you are performing and not creating anxiety about the remaining things that are undone.

3. Use Time Task Balancing

As described previously, this is the ability to set task and project work when you have available time and not trying to cram it into days when you are full of meetings or otherwise busy. It also forces us to look at the days we often get a lot of calls or other interruptions and place our tasks on other days when we can provide focused, and quality, efforts.

4. Plan Before Action

Before jumping in and just getting busy, put a little thought and planning into how you will attack a task or project. Think about it for just a bit, not to the point of overthinking, but a little planning will help the flow and ensure you are on a path to produce an excellent outcome.

5. Double Check Your Work

That little typo in the email might not seem like much to you and it certainly doesn't impact the overall context of your note, but that typo, and small mistakes like it, become a part of your reputation and legacy. Take a small amount of time and check your work before hitting the send button or ordering 100 copies of it for the big meeting. Often this second pass through something will yield minor mistakes that could harm your credibility.

6. Have Someone Else Review Your Work

We tend to review the products we produced through the lens of what we meant to say and not what we actually wrote or even said. Have someone else check your work with independent eyes. This is a great practice, especially for important things.

7. Listen Effectively to Others

Providing quality and excellence in interactions with other people starts with providing focused, and uninterrupted listening. Your mind may be telling you that you have other things going on and to pay attention to the interruptions that are popping up, but you must provide respectful focus to listening to others. You may not have 30 minutes for Aunt Cindy's call, but to produce a quality outcome, you must provide focused time.

Genuine and Transparent Replaces Guarded and Fake

"I have a lot of respect for genuine people. They may not be perfect, but they are not pretending to be."
Anthony Gucciardi

The most admiration, respect, and deepest, most connected relationships will belong to those who choose a path of genuineness and transparency. When we become willing, through a shift in our attitudes and beliefs, to be who we really are and let others see that we will create a relatability that is unmatched. We will create commonality with the other flawed humans in the universe. The connections we have with people will deepen and become stronger as you choose to be the real you.

From the perspective of leadership, both at work and in the home, people will be much more likely followers of the transparent and real than they would be to the fake and false. The strength of your followership will be enhanced by your choices to be genuine and real. Let your team know you have challenges, not in a false bravado, pity me, type of way, but in a real human way. And certainly, never in response to when a team member is expressing a challenge. The same at home. It's great to let the kids know you are having a tough time, tell them of your emotional challenges, and let them know when things aren't great. You are going to build a stronger consensus and team around genuineness than you ever would with your projected perfection.

Genuine People Build Strong Connections with Others

Genuineness and transparency begin with how we choose to communicate with others. Our ability to become real to others is based on how we communicate with them. There are five levels of communication intimacy, and each describes a deeper level of genuineness:

1. Non-Disclosing Safety
This is the level of communication with no transparency, and it is elevator talk. It is the small talk and common greetings that you would share with anyone. There is very little emotional conveyance, and no risk involved. You can have this level of communication intimacy with anyone and everyone.

2. Facts
This type of communication is the sharing of widely established factual data. There is also very little risk here and you can share this with a wide group of people. This is also the most common type of communication in the workplace.

3. Opinions and Values
In this level of communication intimacy, the circle in which you share this with should be smaller. Not everyone will care what you think about any particular subject and some topics such as religion and politics are going to be a non-starter for most people. There is some risk involved when you begin sharing your opinions, no matter how widely held. Here your genuineness and transparency begin to grow.

4. Feelings
Now we are getting to some real transparency and genuineness. This communication level is about sharing how you feel. This should be done with a much smaller group of people and those in which you want to build a relationship built on transparency. There are certainly risks associated with sharing your feelings and we can't always expect other people to understand or validate those feelings.

5. Who You Are and What You Need
This level of communication is the most intimate, most disclosing, and the most transparent. When the real you and what you need is shared in communication, it will create a depth of conversation and relationship that will be strong and lasting. This should only be done with a trusted and select few and the risk of sharing this type of genuineness is high.

Many people, even in long-term relationships, never get past level one or two in their communication and this is reflected in their lack of trust and depth with each other. Even more sad is that many marital or significant other relationships never really get past level three or four. To become true and genuine, we must be able to have level four and five communications with the people closest in our life.

In his groundbreaking book "The Five Dysfunctions of a Team", Patrick Lencioni identified two types of trust: reliable and vulnerable. Reliable trust is based on what you do. If you say you will call me tomorrow by three, and you do, reliable trust is built or maintained. Reliable trust is common, and we will provide it to almost anyone. Reliable trust also has high fluidity in that it can be lost and rebuilt many times over based on performance and what you do. Because of this reliable trust is not very strong.

Much rarer is vulnerable trust which is built on the genuine who you are and not what you do. In my thirty plus years of working with leaders, I have witnessed maybe five executive teams that truly build and utilize vulnerable trust and the results are amazing. As a foundation for teamwork and communication, nothing will be stronger than a base of vulnerable trust. This is also certainly true about all our relationships. When any relationship is built only on reliable trust, it will not be that strong or lasting. Those relationships in which vulnerable trust is a foundation will experience greater depth, longevity, and mutual caring.

Building vulnerable trust is not easy. The process forces us to move past who we want to be and how we want to be seen into the real you. The one with warts and challenges. The one with successes and failures (yes, you have all had some). The person that has fears. The person that does some things well and is challenged by others. The individual that has genuine human frailties and emotions. The person that has experiences that excite them and those that bring them anxiety and sadness. When we choose to share these things with others, we are building vulnerable trust and becoming a much more transparent and genuine person.

One final observation about vulnerable trust and its rarity: even many long-term relationships, including marriages, never get to true vulnerable trust. Many marriages are based solely on what each other does, how they perform, and how they live up to their commitments. Reliable, absolutely; genuine and strong, not nearly so much.

Many people are addicted to who they want to be. What their LinkedIn profile says about them. They view themselves as they have chosen to project their image to others. To the world, they are a series of Photoshopped, AI enhanced, Facebook pictures of the perfect family, the perfect home, ideal pet, and the perfect job. As addicting as those images can be, we all know they are not the truth and not the genuine you. You are not fooling anyone with the false projection of perfection in all aspects of your life. The scary thing is that you have largely bought into these same projections and images. You may not even remember who you really are either.

The first step of adopting an attitude and belief of genuineness is to first really know yourself. Take some time and identify your core values and reconnect with your motivations and motives. Knowing your "why" or remembering your "why" is a powerful first step in reconnecting to the genuine you. My best recommendation, shared relatively recently by a close and loved soul, is to note or journal these. Your "why" is the ultimate target for why you are doing what you do, and your values are the core boundaries and guidelines that you operate by and expect others to operate by as well.

Sometimes, the deep dive into your motivations and motives will be surprising to you. We don't always do things for the altruistic reasons we have hoped.

To continue your self-discovery, remember, and document, things you are good at, things you enjoy doing, things that make you laugh or smile, something that brings you joy, your greatest successes and victories, your biggest failures, your challenges, what you are not good at, your most frequent emotional composition, your insecurities (we all have some), your fears, who and what you need to forgive and heal from, things that cause you anxiety, and things you dislike doing. This process of remembering will reconnect to a big part of who you really are and not what you choose to project to other people.

One quick note about the discovery of fears noted above: on first blush, you will identify some cursory fears like fear of the dark, fear of spiders, fear of heights, etc. Take a longer and more discovering look at this to discover your truly emotionally based fears. Some examples of those include fear of abandonment, fear of failure, fear of success, fear of rejection, and the fear of embarrassment.

Sharing the information you just rediscovered about yourself becomes the next step in your new transparency. Not with everyone and not all at once in one big "this is me" upchuck of data, but in an incremental way in which you can gauge the receptiveness of others and their ability to provide nonjudgemental empathy to your disclosures.

As we become more transparent and genuine, and less guarded and fake, we must also understand some boundaries to our information. Not all people we encounter should be the beneficiaries of our transparency. Our decisions on disclosure should always be based on our role with people and the desire to build deeper rapport and relationships with them. We need to hold some information that will damage our credibility when we are in a leadership role, we need to hold onto some of our challenges when talking with co-workers, we must not disclose certain degrees of genuineness to those who may hold it or use it against us later. The simple rule here is to be transparent but also be smart and use good judgement. Another rule to consider is to be more transparent than you may be initially comfortable with but not so open as to give away everything about you on the second interaction with someone. Build some relationship depth and reliable trust prior to becoming vulnerable and transparent.

To build a more genuine and transparent you, begin to:

1. Discover or Rediscover Yourself
The starting point of greater transparency is knowing yourself or maybe reacquainting you with you. As discussed previously, this requires a deep dive into both the good and the unattractive parts of you to get a clear and balanced version of yourself.

2. Engage Self-Honesty
Be fully honest with yourself. Brutally honest with who you are and not the projection of who you want to be. Don't fall into the trap of being overly self-critical, but be truthful with your strengths and challenges, successes, and failures.

3. Stop Projecting Perfection

That tendency to only share the good news and hide the challenges (thank you Facebook and Instagram) creates the illusion that you are perfect, and all is well. That doesn't mean you should air your dirty laundry on social media, but it does mean you shouldn't try so hard for perfectly filtered and cropped pictures and showing off only the grand parts of your vacation.

4. Get Comfortable Sharing

Start small and incrementally and share some of the details of your life you have previously guarded. Again, make sure you are sharing this with the right circle of people and those with whom you want to build deeper connections. Refer to the communication intimacy and disclosure list and work down from opinions and into feelings and true genuineness.

5. Let Others Share Too

As you begin to share your thoughts, feelings, and experiences, others will want to reciprocate. Make sure you give people the permission, uninterrupted listening, and empathy to do that. You can't be the person that shares your stuff and expect understanding and empathy and but allow that space to others.

6. Apologize

Nothing is quite as transparent and genuine as owning your mistakes and openly apologizing for them. No blame, no excuses, no justifications, no long stories about why you did it; but pure ownership and accountability with a sincere apology.

7. Be Humble
Humility, when combined with genuine confidence, will help you share more of yourself and be more transparent. This value becomes reinforced as you start hearing more transparent information about other people.

8. Address Your Fears
There will be much more about this later but learn to acknowledge and then begin to address your fears. Dealing with your fears involves confronting them, often slowly, and in small steps. Overcoming even a little bit of your fear set will help significantly with your ability to be transparent and genuine.

9. Embrace the Commonalities
One of the greatest side effects of becoming more transparent and genuine is when you discover other people, sometimes those very close to you, have the same type of challenges and issues. They were looking for that common experience empathy, and whether you admit it or not, so were you. Celebrate those "me too" moments when sharing with someone else.

Ownership and Accountability Replaces Blame and Denial

"Wisdom stems from personal accountability. We all make mistakes; own them, learn from them. Don't throw away the lesson by blaming others."
Steve Maraboli

You have to own your own shit. There, I said it.

If you think about it a bit, the people we admire the most and have the most respect for are the ones who accept responsibility for their actions and own everything around them. They don't go to the excuse, justification, or blame well; they simply take accountability for what they have done, the good and the bad.

One of the greatest benefits of accountability is being able to learn the lessons from our mistakes. When we justify them away, or blame them or make excuses, we fail to connect with what we could learn or the lesson the universe is trying to teach us. All our mistakes and challenges should be opportunities to learn new approaches and paths to success. Accountability is not about beating yourself up about a mistake but rather about stepping back and seeing what you need to learn from it.

Likewise with ownership, we learn to use a more entrepreneurial approach with greater creativity and drive, when we choose to own what is happening around us. Whether we can control it, or even influence, owning it provides us with a global view and establishes greater credulity with other people. It can no longer be what the organization did but rather what we did. It is no longer about how he decided but how we decided. We must own our organization, and the choices made by those closest to us. If it is even remotely in your sphere of influence or you represent it somehow (i.e. you are a leader in the organization or the head of the household) you must own the actions, decisions, and choices made. You may not have made the choice personally or even participated in it much, but you still must own it.

Taking Responsibility, Without Any Blame, is a Strong Display of Emotional Intelligence

Currently, a lot of companies and organizations are calling their team members back from remote work associated with the COVID-19 shutdown. These decisions are made at the highest levels of the company and you, the immediate supervisor, had no input into the decision and it even affects you adversely. You're receiving a lot of grumbling and pushback from your team. Some are downright angry. The easy thing to do is to blame "management". The harder and right thing to do is to own the decision and support it as if it was your own.

You want to go a vegan restaurant, the kids want McDonalds, the spouse wants to go to Outback. Despite your wants, the decision is Outback (this is a good compromise and small thing that should not require a fight). The kids are mad. The easy thing is to blame the spouse and tell them to go talk to him or her. The harder, and right thing to do, is proclaim that "we" have decided to go to Outback. Ownership and accountability.

Not too long ago, I let my ego and pride lead me into a field of landmines with a person I admire a respect greatly. My mouth ran amok, and I impulsively reacted to an initial situation and then botched the follow-up conversation badly too. A perfect storm and detailed case study of how not to deal with someone you care about. But I owned it. I apologized for it directly and without any justification or excuse. I was wrong and said so. Now the apology was no guarantee for forgiveness, but it opened the door for that possibility and created a baseline for moving forward.

Especially in the workplace, we seem so committed to justifying our actions, providing excuses for why something didn't happen, and even blaming others. We fear some type of repercussion or consequence if we truly own what we have done and accept accountability. Often those repercussions are entirely a figment of our imagination or based on some ancient history or legend. You will lose more credibility with others by blaming, excuse making, and justifying, than you ever will by owning a mistake you made or from the mistake itself.

One of our larger customers over the years had a very hands-on CEO that was also the company founder. When providing this very large organization with leadership training and coaching, it became clear very quickly that there was a fear of this CEO. It had become even a legend that if you made the wrong misstep or an error and the CEO would personally lead you to the guillotine and lop off your head. It was so pervasive that the leadership team was paralyzed in decision making and they were constantly trying to anticipate what the CEO might think or say. Having heard enough of that, I asked the CEO one day about how many people he had personally terminated for mistakes or errors. The answer was exactly one and that was many years before. This event had become a legend that now an entire leadership team used as a crutch or excuse instead of owning their own decisions. They spent more time covering their backsides than leading others. They had taken blame and excuse making to an all-new level.

A bit smaller organization in the public sector performed the first 360-degree evaluations (survey of team member views and feelings about the culture and leadership quality) of all departments and all leaders. Instead of taking the feedback and turning it into action plans to get better and create a solid working culture, they spent days justifying why the scores were as they were. They justified and blamed instead of learning the lessons that should have been taught.

The lack of accountability and ownership causes significant personal issues as well as those in the workplace. In an interesting morphing, lack of accountability can also turn into gossiping and tattling behaviors which are especially unattractive. A former friend thought it was necessary to take a grievance with me to someone else and even a relative of hers. This person was so avoidant of ownership that they wanted to make sure that their side of the story, with all the requisite exaggerations, was included. So instead of taking accountability and responsibility, they chose a path of pre-spin and pre-damage control to make sure they came out smelling like a rose.

Your initial reaction to accountability and ownership will be that it doesn't feel like much fun. But the truth is, that over time, it becomes a very natural feeling, and very freeing in the sense that you don't always have to scramble for excuses, justifications, and sources to blame. Free yourself by adding more accountability.

To grow your attitude and belief of accountability and ownership, begin to:

1. Spare the Explanation
The moment you feel tempted to add an explanation, especially the ones loaded upfront in a conversation, stop yourself. Explanations are perceived as excuses and justifications by most people, and this will harm your credibility.

2. Look in the Mirror
Likewise, if you are tempted to place blame on someone or something else, look first at the amount of your participation. If, at a minimum, you facilitated it happing, you own it. If you had the ability to choose options, you own it. If you could have seen it coming, you own it. If one of your team or family members, did it or said it, you own it.

3. Use Plural Pronouns

The simple rule is to share credit and take blame. Although this sounds harsh and rather unfair, it is the way it should work. When your team or family accomplishes something good, share the praise and appreciation openly with them. Use plural pronouns (we, they, our, us, their) when speaking of the good. Conversely, use personal pronouns (I, me, mine, I'd) when referring to anything that you need to own that is not good.

4. Acknowledge the Issue and Then Repair It

Ownership is not about creating an environment where you constantly feel regret and being beaten up. Acknowledge the issue or problem, apologize as needed and openly, and then move into repairing the issue quickly. Repairing and making sure the issue doesn't repeat is a stronger part of your lasting image and legacy than the original mistake or misstep ever will be. You will be remembered for the changed behavior and not the original issue.

5. Apologize

Get past your ego block and offer a sincere apology and commitment to fix or not reoccur the issue. Don't use a weak form of apology like "I apologize" or worse yet, "we apologize". Use the ownership form of apology with the highest emotional impact of "I'm sorry". First person and extreme ownership. An apology also demonstrates humility and a desire to move forward. It does not release you from accountability, but it may lessen the blows a bit.

6. Note the Lesson and Plan
Take note of what you learned in any issue or challenge but don't stop there. Make a little bit of an action plan to assist you in not repeating the same mistake again. Some little reminders like "I won't speak when angry", or "I will follow-up more closely with that team member." Nothing elaborate, but just enough action items to keep you from replicating any past failure.

7. Take Care of Your Resilience
Accountability and responsibility require personal resilience and energy. It can be draining to own everything going on around you so you will need to make sure your physical, mental, and emotional resilience skills are in top shape. If you're feeling beaten up and have little resilience, summoning ownership and accountability will be difficult. That is when the excuses and blaming seem to flow naturally out of our mouths.

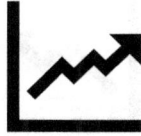

Section IV – Rise!

Now for the really good stuff.

This is where we turn our attention to getting the more happiness we want, the more love we crave, the more enjoyment in life we have been looking for, and the more success we have been hoping for. We rise beyond any challenges from self-defeating behaviors and limiting beliefs and attitudes. We rise above what has been holding us back. We rise to the potential that we have always had inside of us.

We rise.

Movement and Momentum

"For any movement to gain momentum, it must start with a small action."
Adam Braun

A dear soul reminded me recently of the power of creating movement and momentum in the right direction. The physical laws indicate that an object in motion will tend to stay in motion and an object beginning to create momentum will continue that momentum with growth.

As it is with us. As we start, we will create forward growth movement and momentum. This is not about tackling seven behaviors and four attitudes and beliefs all at once. This is about creating the momentum from working on one thing. The important piece is we commit and start. From there, the work forward will be easier to add to and continue.

Likewise with forward movement, standing still creates more standing still and creating movement from an entrenched idle position becomes much harder. With an ever-changing world, standing still equates to moving backwards.

We also must adopt the mantra of when to rise. We need to rise when we are down. We need to rise when things are okay. We need to rise when things are great. This is about creating movement and momentum no matter where we are at. Rising creates more rising and that rising is likely to continue. In short, we need to create rising and growth momentum as a constant.

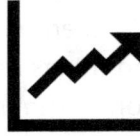

Proportionality and Planning

"For any movement to gain momentum, it must start with a small action."
Adam Braun

I know the tendency exists to look at the list of self-defeating and limiting behaviors, and the roster of attitudes and beliefs and feel like you have a lot of work to do. It may seem daunting to you. It may even seem overwhelming.

Please, let's achieve some balance before we go to work. You are in a great spot. You have more than most people on earth. You are loved. You are cared for. You have a job. Your food source and housing are secure. You do far more right than not. You have achieved a great deal in your life. Remind yourself of this and maybe read this again and again until you believe it.

We are now going to embrace the IPA journey. No, not beer.

I	Identify
P	Prioritize
A	Attack

Now we are going to do some triage work and begin to apply some strategies. Look back at the listing and scoring of the self-defeating and self-limiting behaviors and find the ones that impact you the most. We are going to be looking for the top three and a great formula and scoring grid to use is:

Frequency:
Often	10 Points
Occasionally	5 Points
Never	0 Points

Impact:
Often	10 Points
Occasionally	5 Points
Never	0 Points

Then multiply the frequency by the impact (F X I) and you will produce a self-defeating and self-limiting behavior overall score that will range from 100 at its highest to 0 at its lowest.

See the Rise! Workbook for worksheets and examples to help you with this.

At this point, we can clearly see the three greatest drags on our happiness and success. Note these top three and note three to four action plan items for each of them. This is a listing of what you are doing to do, beginning today to reduce and eliminate these behaviors that do not serve you well.

We are going to do the same by choosing one attitude and belief that you want to embrace moving forward. One belief set, attitude, or mindset, which may replace a poorly serving attitude or belief or one that drives some of our self-defeating behaviors. Here again, you will want to note some action plan steps to get there and begin the process of mentally locking into and focusing about this attitude and belief.

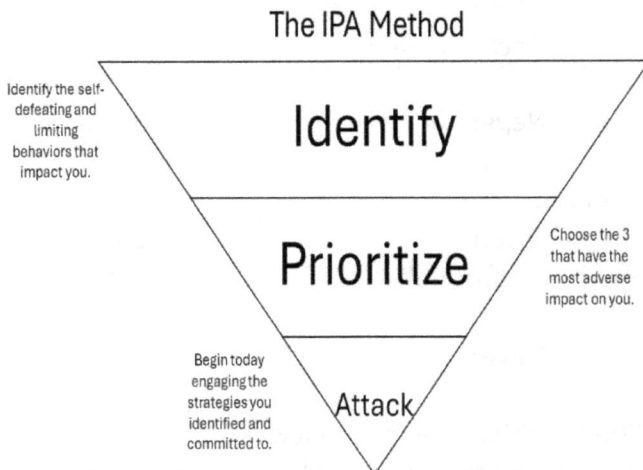

The IPA Method

Identify the self-defeating and limiting behaviors that impact you.

Identify

Prioritize

Choose the 3 that have the most adverse impact on you.

Begin today engaging the strategies you identified and committed to.

Attack

Only after you have mastered and resolved to your satisfaction the big three self-defeating behaviors, can you add another, and only if you have another of high impact. Our focus will be on the behaviors and beliefs that hold us back the most and not ones that show up only on Thanksgiving in odd numbered years.

We must note the humanity involved in behavioral change. In and of itself, changing a behavior is easy. We can do that almost instantly with a little thought and intention. What is harder is to sustain behavioral change and make it a lasting habit and a part of who we are. That is where attitudinal and belief alignment come into play. As we align our attitudes and beliefs and, in some cases, completely substitute new positive beliefs and attitudes, the sustainment of our new and better behaviors will seem natural. Our attitudes and beliefs drive our behaviors. We approach the behaviors and attitudes at the same time for maximum impact for you.

Our last step is the one referenced earlier. Start. Begin the process of engaging your strategies and get these behaviors reduced and produce awesome driving attitudes.

Another human dynamic to note is our failure moments and setbacks. We will not execute our plans for changed behaviors and attitudes and beliefs perfectly. We will have those moments when we pause and say to ourselves "why did I do that? I know better" or "why did I say that? I sure shouldn't have". This is perfectly normal, perfectly human, and part of how adults learn. This is about learning from the great use of new behaviors and embrace of better attitudes and beliefs and correcting ourselves gently when we err. Success in addiction recovery is measured by the frequency of relapses and the time between those relapses. So, it is with your behavioral changes. As you relapse back into self-defeating and self-limiting behaviors, we want to measure that it is happening less frequently and the time between these minor setbacks is getting longer and longer.

We must also show ourselves some grace when we don't execute perfectly. Yes, we are going to go back to some old, and not useful, behaviors. We are not always, at least initially, going to be able to produce a great attitude for the day. It's okay. You're human. Give yourself some grace. Note the setback, learn from it, forgive yourself quickly, and continue your forward progress.

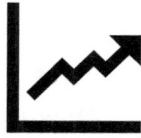

Progress and Journaling

"Progress is impossible without change, and those who cannot change their minds cannot change anything."
George Bernard Shaw

Tracking your progress, in any endeavor, is an important part of fully realizing our goals. Although there is still a stigma with journalling, it is the most practical way to note your progress, document your goals, describe any setbacks, and provide observations about the impact of your progress.

We have incorporated journalling elements, forty days' worth, into Rise! The Workbook. You can also use a $1.19 spiral notebook with the same impact.

Here is a great blueprint for what to journal each day:

1. Gratitude
As much as you're probably a little tired of hearing about gratitude, here it is again. Note in your daily journal five things that you are thankful for that day or from the prior day. Asterisk two of them; one to purposefully share with another person and one in which you are grateful for something you did.

2. Attitude Intention
Note the attitude that you want to embrace for the day.
Do this is very simple form and only use a word or two.
This becomes your intention word for the day, and you can
use it as a reminder mantra.

3. Behavior Focus
Briefly note the three prevalent behaviors that you want to
work on today or that you worked on yesterday.

4.   Progress Score or Grade
Give yourself a score on your behaviors and attitude for
the day. We have been wired for achievement, and some
of us for competition, and this is a healthy way to create a
trail of our progress. It doesn't matter if you use a letter
grade, percentage, or a raw number. It creates a baseline
to measure tomorrow against. Two things to remember:
you are only competing against yourself and trying to be
better tomorrow than you were today and be generous
with yourself. If it was good, give it a B. If it was extra-
good, give it an A.

5. Note Any Challenges
Without belaboring it, note any challenging situations or
times when you slipped back into old habits and behaviors.
This is good to note as you self-manage moving forward.

6. Forgiveness
Note anyone or anything that you need to forgive and the date in which you will do so.

Since you're going to track and monitor your progress, you should also build in some celebrations and rewards too. No impulsiveness for a week, buy yourself an ice cream cone or a beer. No overthinking for a month, take yourself to lunch at your favorite place. These little rewards for a job well done are important reinforcements for your behavioral and attitudinal changes.

Embrace New Habits

"Motivation is what gets you started. Habit is what keeps you going."
Jim Ryun

Habits are those small actions done repetitively that drive our results and outcomes. Our attitudes and beliefs dictate our habits and our behaviors both support them and are supported by them. All of us could produce a listing of bad, and sometimes even mortally significant habits but for us, we are going to embrace a new set of habits designed to support our positive attitudes and beliefs and reduce the drag of any self-defeating or limiting behaviors.

For me, habits have been crucial to my success in certain areas. The habits of writing (a break is coming), working out, getting up early, do pushups, answer emails at a specific time, show appreciation, use courtesy, pay bills on a weekly basis, and to always say goodnight to those I love, have served me very well. Equally well serving are the elimination or reduction of bad habits that did not serve me or support my desired outcomes. I also engaged in the tracking of many of these until they became locked into my behavioral patterns and got some great daily feedback about how I was doing with them.

I truly tried to make the following list into a clever acronym but epically failed. Below are a great set of habits to embrace that will serve you well. These are the habits we want to engage to create the success and happiness we desire and deserve:

1. Communicate

Communicate frequently, transparently, and well. Listen, manage your tone, watch your non-verbal signals, and speak in-person when possible. Communication is the foundation for trust, teamwork, relationships, your image, and leadership.

2. Pause

Get used to taking a two to three second pause before responding, reacting, speaking, or typing. This pause allows you to compose your emotional composition, choose words that serve you and don't hurt you, and check for unintended consequences.

3. Move

Whether physical movement or headway towards the completion of a project or task, move. Act and stop overthinking it. Movement, exercise, and getting up early will serve your behaviors and attitudes and beliefs well.

4. Forgive

Life is far too short to carry around a bunch of unforgiven wrongs and it is only hurting you. Provide genuine forgiveness and don't let the event impact future interactions or behaviors.

5. Give

Give generously of your times and talents but never to the point of overextension or being overwhelmed. Giving certainly helps others but has a great impact on you as well. Make it a habit and not an exception.

6. Open

The world is full of opportunities waiting to be experienced and full of information that will help us learn and grow. All we have to do is be open to those things. Openness reduces our tendency to be harshly judgmental of people and far more accepting of shortcomings.

7. Kindness

In a world filled with harsh, mean, and cruel actions, you can stand out nicely by simply being kind. Often kindness is best expressed as an absence of meanness and malice. Don't be mean to people. Don't hurt them. Don't cut people out of your life. Even the hardest and most difficult news can be delivered with compassion. Be known as a consistently kind soul.

8. Polite

The use of please, thank you, I'm sorry, excuse me, and the like are sadly rarer than they should be. Use the words of courtesy, if nothing more than out of habit.

9. Respect

Respect, like courtesy, kindness, and politeness, is sorely lacking in the modern workplace, at home, and in society. We have the unique opportunity to change that by being respectful to everyone, no matter if they can do anything for you or not, no matter if they have wronged you or not, no matter if you will never see them again; be respectful. The easiest ways to demonstrate respect are to provide uninterrupted listening, show some interest in them, and always use courtesy.

10. Appreciate

When someone has done something well, tell them. When you appreciate the work, they have done, or the way the house looks, tell them. Take just a nanosecond out of the universe and express your gratitude in real time as you witness it.

These habits, although not curative of everything, will certainly support long-term sustainability in your positive attitudes and beliefs and help with producing the behaviors you desire, and not the ones that limit you.

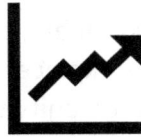

Share Your Journey and Get Feedback

"Anything is possible when you have the right people there to support you."
Misty Copeland

Again, the credit here belongs to Dr. Marshall Goldsmith. He opened this door, and I can only hope to amplify what he has previously written.

If you have ever wanted someone to notice something about you but they did not, you understand the value of sharing your journey. We need to tell a few people in our life what we are going to be working on. That way, they can become our cheerleader, coach, supporter, and feedback partner. This loop of feedback is invaluable. They will encourage and cheer when we are doing well and encourage and remind us of when we have stumbled. Again, this is priceless assistance to our behavioral changes.

Many journeys for sustained behavioral change, even though they have started strong, failed because of a lack of a support network. You can create this powerful team by just sharing what you are going to be working on and requesting their help and feedback.

This is not about sending out a group email to your 20 team members and fifty friends or making a Facebook post to your 500-plus followers. This is about selecting a few people that know you well, that have good intentions and a motive to truly help you, and people who have enough relationship depth to be truthful with you. These two or maybe three people will be your own personal coaching staff and cheer squad.

When you are not hearing much from your small circle, you will have to ask for some feedback. Ask how you are doing. Ask what they are seeing. Ask specific pointed questions about behaviors and attitudes and beliefs. Never pushback on the feedback and always just thank them for the input.

If you have a feedback partner in your life, cherish him or her and hold them extremely close to you. These people are priceless. Feedback partners are those people who, with a combination of honesty and compassion, tell you how you are doing. They share the good and they share the bad, but with a deep caring for you and your success and happiness. Their motivation is only to help you and never to hurt or embarrass you. If you don't have one of these people in your life, they are probably closer than you think and probably just an ask away.

Apologies, Fixes, and Forgiveness

"Even things that look broken beyond repair have a chance at being whole again."
Natasha Preston

There is a high (read as certainty) that some of your self-defeating and self-limiting behaviors, and poor attitude and belief choices have had an adverse impact on others. The good news is that everything, sans death, is fixable, if we swallow our pride and ego, and work towards a resolution.

Here is a great opportunity for us to try out our new attitude of ownership and accountability. As a first step, we must acknowledge what we have done, the impact it had, and who was impacted by our behavior or attitude. From there, we get to practice another great attitude and belief set, humility and confidence. We must apologize, in the correct form that has been described above. Not to groups but to all individuals that were adversely affected. This comes from a position of combined strength and total humility. We may even have to ask for forgiveness and a clean slate to work from. Again, this is no guarantee they will provide forgiveness, and some people profess to forgive while still allowing the transgression to impact interactions.

The apology alone will not guarantee any repair, but it does bring us to at least a zero-point with the people affected. They may not even accept our apology, but it is important we offer it and offer it sincerely.

Next, we have a couple of paths for repair. The first, and most obvious repair is the sustained and long-term change in your attitude, beliefs, and behaviors. An apology without a change in these areas is useless. People must see the changes in you for the apology to resonate and their forgiveness to flow. The second area where fixing is necessary is where something tangible can be repaired. Is there a notation in an HR file that was written impulsively? Did you say something to someone that prevented a promotion? Did you make a harsh comment on social media? Did your boorish behavior ruin lunch? Did your pride cause you to lash out and cause a rift between a couple? Everything broken can be repaired and should be. This demonstration is as important and an apology and changed behavior. If you can make it right, you must strive to do so.

Finally, we must be willing to provide true forgiveness (where we don't let the wrong or hurt impact future interactions) to those that have wronged us and to the mistakes that we have made ourselves. Self-forgiveness is often the most difficult to muster but as important as any provided to other people. Forgive openly and freely and note any needed forgiveness in your journal or log.

Address Your Fears

"One of the greatest discoveries a man makes, one of his greatest surprises, is to find he could do what he was afraid he couldn't do."
Henry Ford

Fears come in all shapes and sizes. Some scholarly works identify well over 200 significant fears carried by adults. For our purpose, we need to work on and reduce the impact of deeply rooted emotional and ego-based fears. We are going to ignore entirely the fear of snakes, spiders, the dark, big dogs, and fire. You can deal with those all on your own.

When unmanaged and untamed, fears can have a significant impact on our ability to grow and move forward. They are the stunting of many good intentions to build new behaviors and enhanced beliefs and attitudes. They impact us without ever telling us that they are coming. We know they are there but seldom realizing the impact of fears until opportunities have passed us by. They prevent us from deeper connections and relationships, they keep us from experiencing new things, and they hold us in a pattern of comfortable inaction. We all have fears, but very happy and successful people have actively managed them and put many of them in abeyance, so they no longer impact their life.

The common element in the elimination of fears is facing them. Summoning the courage to put yourself in the situation and trusting your confidence and resilience enough to pull you through the experience you were afraid of. Not in one big jump (although that works too) but rather in some small doses at first and increasing your comfort in dealing with the situation or people involved. We must take on the fear and gradually add to our confidence in taking on bigger and bigger things that scare us.

The fears that we want to spend some time on and really identify their impact are the ones rooted deeply in our emotional composition and egos. They are the ones that keep us from reaching our highest levels of success and happiness. Those fears include:

1. Failure
We must reconnect with our successes and develop confidence in our path towards success, both on a macro level, and with individual projects and relationships.

2. Abandonment and Rejection
Here again a reconnection is needed but this time to those who accept us and choose to stay connected with us. We must appreciate those people openly and work to keep them connected and accepting of us. This fear can also be expressed as a fear of loneliness or being alone. This is easily tackled by building more connections, getting out more, and learning to utilize your alone time productively and towards your purpose.

3. Embarrassment and Explanation

This is one of the most unreasonably built fears identified and concocted only in the dark chambers of our minds. No one, and I mean no one, has ever perished or even suffered great harm from a little embarrassment or having to explain an action. Some people are so paralyzed by this that they will jeopardize relationships to avoid any explanation to others. Develop confidence in who you are and what your choices have been. If you can justify the choice or decision to yourself, you can explain it to others.

4. Loss

This one is interesting because it can be connected to the loss of life, the loss of a loved one, or the loss of a relationship. We must provide ourselves with two reminders: the first is about our mortality; we will perish when we are supposed to, and others around us are mortal as well. We must also be very intentional and mindful about living exactly in the current moment. A live that moment fully because tomorrow is not guaranteed, for you or anyone else.

5. Autonomy

The fear of any type of burden or restriction, or even in some cases, added responsibility, can be a fear factor in some people. They bristle openly about anything they did not individually adopt as a responsibility. We must remind ourselves that with success, growth, and relationships, responsibility and accountability come along. It is part of the equation, and we must develop comfort with it.

6. Success

This one always strikes people as odd and evokes a lot of smartass comments too. The fear of success is real, and some people hide behind this fear when ignoring opportunities and possibilities. Overcoming this fear requires an acceptance of the abundance, in tangible and intangible ways, and reminding ourselves that we are worthy of the success, and we worked hard to get there.

6. Invisibility

The fear of being ignored or being irrelevant or being forgotten can all be summed up in this category. The curative part of this fear is to speak up, be heard, and to produce something memorable that will be constantly associated with you.

As shared briefly before, the keys to overcoming our fears include:

1. Awareness and Acknowledgement

Back off your ego a bit, spend some time reflecting, and identify those fears that hold you back. We all have them, and a little feedback may help you here as well. Also note the impacts that those fears have on your life and growth.

2. Face the Fears

Begin with small steps until the fear becomes buried permanently. Take on the opportunities that fear is currently holding you back from. One step at a time.

3. Challenge the Negative Attitudes
Fears will drive and certainly reinforce many of the negative attitudes and beliefs we have identified in this book. When you feel one of those negative belief sets or attitudes creeping in, take it on and replace it with a desired attitude immediately4.

4. Focus on Positive Outcomes and Possibilities
Continuously remind yourself of the positive outcomes and positive expectations that will occur when you overcome a fear or two. Even note the benefits if that helps remind you. You will discover there are a big list of possibilities when we are open to them.

Working on our fears is not a ton of fun but certainly very rewarding and necessary for us to achieve the happiness and success we desire.

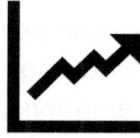

Manage and Build Your Emotions

"Emotions can get in the way or get you on the way."
Mavis Mazhura

Our emotions and our emotional composition will drive our attitudes and beliefs which in turn drive our behaviors. Every behavior you display can be traced back directly to your current or most prevalent emotional composition.

Most adults have limited awareness of their emotional awareness. They certainly know when they are angry or upset, but don't really know much more than that. Emotional awareness is a powerful part of knowing yourself and when you engage in managing your emotional composition, you can become unstoppable.

Emotionally healthy people experience a wide range of emotions regularly. They can have days with joy, overwhelm, frustration, and satisfaction, and that is all perfectly normal. We also have a prevalent emotional state in which we spend the most time daily. That is the one in which we will be applying the work. We need the increased emotional energy from raising our emotional composition to help us sustain our positive attitudes and beliefs and the behaviors we want to project. With poor emotional composition, we will fallback into negative attitudes and self-defeating behaviors.

Our emotions and emotional composition will fall into one of two general categories. Negative, or draining emotions, are driven by fear and positive emotions, the ones that give us that extra spark and bit of life are driven by love. Fear and love are the base emotional drivers. With a greater commitment to love, your emotions will be more positive. More concentration on fear, and your emotional composition will be negative.

This is an exercise in which self-honesty is critical. Many of us, on first blush, would automatically choose an emotional state in the positive, love-based range. Unfortunately, that first pass is more likely where you would like to be and not where you are. Our experience tells us that people likely overestimate (to the positive side) their emotional state by one to two full levels. Be critical and think hard about where you are.

The first step of managing our emotional composition is to track where you are at. The below emotional guidance scales will help you and you will want to record your high point, low point, and most common emotional composition spot for about two weeks. That will give you a pretty good idea of where your most common emotional state is at.

Emotional Composition

0	• Boredom
-15	• Pessimism
-30	• Frustration
-45	• Overwhelm
-60	• Anger
-75	• Hate
-90	• Jealous
-100	• Despair

FEAR

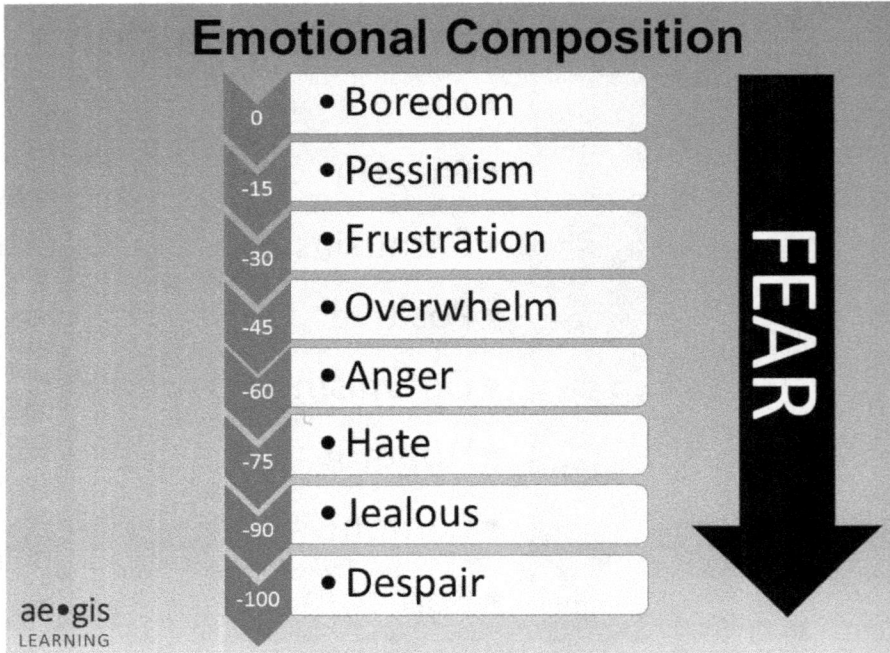

Now that we know where we are at, and we acknowledge we want to move it up, even if it is in the positive range already, we want to use these strategies:

1. Meditate

Believe me, I have heard all the objections for this one. Meditation works and it is your chance to clear your head, gain greater focus, listen to your mind and the universe, and create a great path for the day.

Star small with a target of only a few minutes. Concentrate on your breathing. Breathe the good in through your nose and the bad out from your mouth. Nice deep slow breaths. Sit comfortably and alone and quietly. No need for music and certainly no interruptions. Clear your mind as best you can. Listen to your mind. Stay exactly in the moment you are in. Acknowledge your feelings. Add your intention word for the day, multiple times.

There! You have meditated. Work on extending the time and adding elements to it as needed. Use guided meditation guides as needed. Return to meditation when you are feeling a little strained or stressed during the day. Set a time every day that is your meditation time.

2. Practice Gratitude

3. Forgive and Heal

4. Give

5. Laugh, Play, and Have Fun

We all want to have some fun in our lives, but we often put it in the "when time allows" bucket or we compromise what we enjoy doing for the family or another person. We need to prioritize our fun and schedule it. If you enjoy hiking, put a calendar entry for a few hours on the weekend to hike. Don't give the time away and don't be swayed into another activity. If you enjoy comedy clubs, make a monthly date with yourself and go. Laughter and enjoyment lighten your emotional composition and raise it significantly.

6. Know Your Why, Live Your Why

7. Move and Take Care of Yourself

Challenge Your Definition of Success

"Define success on your own terms, achieve it by your own rules, and build a life you're proud to live."
Anne Sweeney

"Success: To laugh often and love much; to win the respect of intelligent persons and the affection of children;

to earn the appreciation of honest citizens and endure the betrayal of false friends;

to appreciate beauty; and find the beauty in others;

to leave the world a bit better, whether by a healthy child, a garden patch or a redeemed social condition;

to have played and laughed with enthusiasm and sung with exaltation;

to know that even one life breathed easier because you have lived –

this is to have succeeded."
Ralph Waldo Emerson

The final stop in our work to create more happiness and more of what you want is to challenge how we view success.

Far too often, we look at things or the quantifiable. We look at money. We fixate on the accumulation of material objects. We focus on the pieces that other people may see. As we presented earlier, comparisons can kill joy and create a cycle of constantly wanting more things. Perpetually chasing the bigger house, newer car, retirement date, or investment balance. Unfortunately, none of those create long-term happiness or true success.

Do not get me wrong; we need money. We need to survive, and I want you to survive comfortably and without worrying about when you can make the mortgage payment. The shift that I want you to consider is that money and the other standard measures of success are a byproduct of success and not success itself. True success should be measured and worked towards in terms of happiness, satisfaction, and helpfulness to others. If those become your standard of success, the money and other tangible items you desire will follow. It really will.

Years ago, I openly chased money, job titles, organizational power, influence, notability, new cars, and zip codes. Although I was successful in obtaining those things, I was miserable. I was not really a good person to be around. Driven to the point of ignoring important things like relationships, children, self-care, and having any amount of fun. And when the things I desired were achieved, I wanted more. A vice president title needed to be replaced with a senior vice president title. The new 4-Runner had to be replaced with a newer truck. The house now had to be in a gated community. More and more and more and more miserable along the way. Constantly striving for what I thought was success. The day I let those things go and when I shifted my success definition was among the happiest of my life. Although I still appreciate the other measures of success, they have become a byproduct of a better guiding definition of success for me.

The Ralph Waldo Emerson quote above will give us a great deal of hints and clues about how we need to shift our definition and belief of success. Ultimately, success should be measured in terms of your happiness and contentment with who you are. We further want to reduce the timeframe associated with labeling yourself as a success. Many times, we look at long-term measures (a particular dollar amount, a new vehicle next year) as success targets. I want us to shift our success definition to daily. We are going to begin looking at each day as being successful, and the cumulative effect will be a successful career and life.

For that purpose, we have developed a group of success litmus questions to ask yourself at the end of every day. These questions reinforce that you are successful today, tomorrow, and everyday thereafter.

1. Did You Make Your Life Better Today?
Even the simplest thing will work here. Did you do something to improve your life? Maybe clean something? Put some things away? Rearranged something for greater efficiency?

2. Did You Help Someone Today?
This too can be something simple. Did you help anyone that made their day better or easier? Maybe fold their laundry? Smile at them and offer some kindness? The one rub on this one is to never do harm.

3. Did You Laugh and Smile Today?
A smile and a laugh can have a huge impact on your demeanor and support your chosen attitude set. Find something that makes you smile or laugh and make sure you engage in that activity.

4. Did You Learn Something Today?
This is a great barometer of a successful day. Did you learn something new and different? This helps both your attitude and your mind.

5. Did You Do Something for Yourself Today?
We close with a little selfishness. Did you do something for you? This could be a meditation moment, a small break, some self-care, working out, or just enjoying some quiet time. This personal satisfaction is priceless for your attitude management.

Final Encouragement

"I sometimes fell short of being the best, but I never fell short of giving it my best."
William McRaven

I want you to be happier than you have ever been. I want you to achieve the success that you want and have dreamed of. I want your relationships to be deeply connected and meaningful. I want your life to be filled with the potential that you have inside of you.

You can absolutely do this. Choose your top three self-defeating and self-limiting behaviors. Choose the one major attitude and belief you want to embrace and have drive your behaviors. You can track your progress and journal every day. You can attack your fears and work on your emotional composition. I know you can.

I believe in you, and I look forward to hearing about your happiness and success.

Tim

About Tim Schneider

Tim Schneider is a published author, speaker, training facilitator, and executive coach with over 30 years of experience in delivering impactful learning about leadership, teamwork, professional success, and personal growth. His prior works include **_LeadWell: The Ten Competencies of Outstanding Leadership_**, **_Beyond Engagement_**, and **_A Heart for Leadership_**. His work has taken him to every state in the nation and multiple international destinations. Tim remains one of the most sought-after speakers, training facilitators, and coaches in the United States.

Personally, Tim makes his home in Southern Nevada and is the proud dad of two grown boys. He continues his pursuit of a big-time professional contract by playing men's adult league baseball. He also enjoys all outdoor activities, spends time working out, and loves the time with the people closest to him.

Resources

Look for the RISE! Workbook on Amazon or at www.discoveraegis.com.

To learn more about the DiSC assessment, please visit: https://discoveraegis.com/disc/.

www.ingramcontent.com/pod-product-compliance
Lightning Source LLC
Chambersburg PA
CBHW060042100426
42742CB00014B/2672